A HARVEST OF YEARS

My Story, 1876 On-ward

Iva Wilson

ABT, LLC

D1316785

A HARVEST OF YEARS

My Story, 1876 On-ward

Iva Wilson
First Edition
Copyright © 2020 Laur Cabin Trust

ISBN: 978-1-7346692-0-6 (Paperback)

Library of Congress Control Number: 2020903224

Editor: Scott Taylor
Co-Editor: Brandon Taylor
Cover Design: Rudi Hartono

Printed in the United States of America.

Published by:
ABT, LLC
1740 E. Fairview Ave. PMB #100
Meridian, Idaho 83642

ANYTHING NOT SAVED WILL BE LOST.

———— ◆ ————

*This book is dedicated to Iva Cochran-Wilson
and Mary Joan Cochran-Laur.*

Contents

Editor's Preface

She greets you at her door with a graceful smile, appreciative that family would come to visit. That is my last memory of Iva Cochran-Wilson. A frail woman living out her golden years with her daughter Kathleen in their north-end home in Boise, Idaho. She was certainly a favorite of my mother's, Mary "Joan" Cochran-Laur. I would say that the affection between Mother and Aunt Iva was mutual and obvious even for a young boy to witness. You see, Iva was the sister of Ray Cochran, Joan's father, who was lost to cancer when she was an infant. I believe she saw Aunt Iva as her only real opportunity to learn more about her father and his family history. It must have been Joan's curiosity that moved Aunt Iva to hand over her prized Underwood typewriter to her niece, along with the autobiography Iva had pulled from its keys.

For many decades my mother held this book dearly and shared its passages with family and friends. Now we would like to share it with you. As you read this book you should note that the vernacular may seem a little foreign, but that was the way people spoke then. Also, by today's reading standards, the stories lack a smooth transition as you turn through the pages. That being the case, it was important to our family that the stories be received in the same stream of consciousness as they were written on that typewriter, word-for-word in 1960. With Iva's book now in your hands, I hope that you will enjoy her unique perspective as she recounts a life well lived. So if you please, we invite you to begin Iva's story and turn the page.

–Scott Taylor

CHAPTER I

The Pilgrimage

(1960)

————— ◆ —————

This is a story of Iowa, North Dakota and Idaho, a story of their people and their ways of life. Starting with Iowa, the Iowa of at least eighty–five years ago, Iowa today is perhaps the most productive and progressive state in the Union for its size. To me with its rolling hills and wooded streams, it is strangely beautiful. It is a good country to come from and even better to go back to. It is a land of memories intermingled with a past romantic and alluring mystically so it seems, but a past that has gone forever.

It is a homely, friendly sort of a country too– its great prairies and hills furred with summer's smile and pale with temper stamped on her winter floors– winds howling like hungry wolves one moment, and then soughing the old weathered trees swaying with a sonorous restless rhythm.

I lived there over thirty–five years and have been away fifty; when I went back for a visit, there weren't many changes. My town, Gutherie Center, was a tiny town when I lived there and it is still tiny. I think they told me they had gained five hundred souls in that length of time.

Great waves of memories surged over me–happy, poignant, lonely and sad. When you go back to re–explore your own country, you are likely to find dreams and memory all mixed up with solid reality. When I went to this one particular spot in the state, where I had spent my restless girlhood, I wanted to see just what the years had done to it, and if in it, I had learned what the years had done to me. Well, that is what naturally happens when you go on a Pilgrimage.

The little country schools, where I had taught the three R's so faithfully, were still standing with no change whatever and the schoolhouse where I had attended my first school at the tender age of four years (we were sent with older brothers and sisters then) and the old farm my father owned and operated, seemed unchanged– possible a coat of paint or two down the years. The same old house, some old outbuildings ready to topple over and the same old rutty wagon road was still there. Such a mildew of loneliness engulfed me as I stood there really listening for the old sound. A cowbell in the distance, Mother calling the chicks for their soaked cornmeal, the clip–clop of horses coming home from work to the six ears of corn in their feed box and timothy hay. There were the old sagging fences we used to jaywalk over on the snow on our way to school.

When you go back to the place you knew when you were young, you see it through eyes that were especially conditioned; you cannot be objective about it without you trying to write about your background and find you are really writing about yourself. What you owe the land where you were reared is something you can't quite explain. For what you think and feel while very small, never quite leaves you. I think I was trying to recapture something that was unattainable, a dream I think that I was always pursuing but never quite caught up with.

In the town, ghosts walked the narrow streets with me and beside me. Dear faces long since returned to dust were with me and the kindly voices kept me company as I gazed at the lovely old hills. The still quiet moonlight night's perfumes floating upward bewitching the air, night whispers drawn outward like soft silvery music, like no place else on earth. Even the old trees were reaching out their shadowy hands to welcome me back.

CHAPTER II

The Old Homestead

(1876 On-ward)

◆

My first memory of the old homestead was riding over the hills in a farm wagon covered up snugly by an old patched comforter. My mother clutched me closely to her and my brother Roy, was also clinging to her, while Father was busy with the brakes and firmly holding on the lines as we bumped and swayed over the rough roads. We were all in the old spring seat, which kept slipping back and forth, and we went in the valley only to start climbing the next moment. You see my parents were from the plains of Illinois and were not used to hills. Me screaming, "the Ribber, The Ribber" didn't help matters much, as I thought we were heading into a river. Iowa was so new then. My grandfather was the first relative to leave the gentle plains of Illinois for this newer country, Iowa. What fantastic tales he brought back to the waiting folks in Illinois. Like, he has seen "a cabbage six feet tall, a gander too, that was six feet-two and saw a house that covered four-acres."

Our town was six miles away from our farm, squatting on the riverbank like a big content frog. On the edge of the river and back a rod or two were brave trees with toes dug in leaning against the wind. The river lay dimpled by fat rain it seemed every time we drove by. Every one of those days were as friendly as lost puppies. Everyone tried and sincerely too, to make everyone else feel at home. And they all needed that assurance for most of them were far from friends and relatives.

At home, Roy, my brother, and myself had to invent our own amusements and play. We made pets of all things, even tried to get close enough to a rattler to tame it, but our faithful old dog Shep, took the fangs that were meant for us.

Father came on the run when mother screamed and grabbed the always present wad of chewing tobacco from his mouth and applied it to old Shep and with careful nursing we did manage to save her. How we all loved her! I'll never forget how we found her, in an old abandoned shanty. There she was standing knee-deep in puppies, cold and hungry. We bundled the whole family into our wagon and took her home to our warm barn with Ginger and Kate, our two big Clydesdales horses to help keep them warm.

Roy and I were never bored. We were busy from morning till night- wading snow, making snowballs, staging a fight that became real now and then, and begging mother to make us ice-cream. Busy as she was, she would go out and scoop up fresh snow and mix it with rich cream and a bit of sugar. I am sure we enjoyed it more than we do the lovely ice cream concoctions of today with all their varied and fancy goo-goo names. We were very seldom sick and if a cold did threaten, mother fried big red onions rich with brown sugar and gave us the onion syrup or a poultice of onions on our chest. Sometimes if she thought it serious, the ever-present skunk oil or goose oil was applied with hot flannels on our chest. Of course, we always wore the sack of "fetty", smelling to high heaven and supposed to keep away all disease. Our medicine chest always contained skunk oil, goose oil, Camphor and always horse liniment for bruises and aches. A doctor just didn't come to our house. In the spring along with new calves and pigs, we were doused with sulphur and molasses and sassafras tea. A bath on Saturday night was always in the old wooden washtub beside the kitchen stove and the water heated in the big iron teakettle. Later on the new stove, we had a reservoir on the back of the stove and were we proud of our new status in the neighborhood. It took so little those days to make one happy.

Father made us bob sleds not only to ride on, but small ones for our dolls. I cut out women and girls from the old butterick patterns and pinned on new dresses daily. In the summer it was mud pies, playhouses under trees or in the empty corncrib, dressing up in Mother's long skirts and when tired of that we could always splash in the old mud hole when it wasn't occupied by our pigs. At milking time we would hurry out to the cow yard for milking time. Father would squirt the milk from the cow's teat into our mouths and then old Shep would hold her mouth open for her squirt of milk. How about sanitation problems in those days? As I said we were as healthy as the newborn calves.

I remember our first Christmas. We had no tree but Mother turned our little wooden high chair upside down and hung our home knit stockings on each leg. She strung popcorn over each round and in each stocking was a lonely orange and three sticks of horehound candy and a square of maple sugar. Also, two pairs of knitted mittens were there and also some wristlets for Father. We did not lack good things for our dinner, when it was roast goose with all the goodies that go with it. Those geese had nipped our legs so often that we really devoured them with relish. It is the holiday dinner and the memories I still savor in our dear old kitchen as it was, its spicy pies, bright shimmer of jellies, simmering chili sauce and Indian relish. Our table bearing snowdrifts of mash potatoes, piled high in big old bowls, butter oozing down the sides of the white potatoes, a rich-shining gravy on a sea of white tablecloth and the very center the goose or the turkey. I am so grateful for the mellow harvests at winter's eve, for the lingering warmth of Indian summer or the snow flurried and ice-laced borders of our steams and the kindness in people's hearts. Oh, how I miss it all now!

We always looked forward to butchering time. Great barrels of hot water were tipped at just the right angle to slide the big hogs in and out of the hot water until the hair was thoroughly scalded, and then, with our little knives we would help scrape the hog until they were clean and shiny. Then Mother would be busy, headcheese to make, big crooks of mincemeat, rendering of the lard, pickling of the feet and making souse of the ears. She saved the cracklings for our cornbread. I think she used all of the hog but the squeal. Father made the salt brine using saltpeter for some reason. He would cut the hog in chunks and place or pack each piece in the brine. When salty enough to use, Mother would bring up one of the chunks and soak overnight and slice it thick for our meals, great slabs of it with vegetables, and worlds of potatoes and sometimes with fried mush. I can still taste her homemade sausage and the sage. Father and the hired man stored her food away as fast as she could prepare it and so could Roy and I, especially her cornmeal hotcakes and buttermilk biscuits—delicious! We always used big plaid tablecloths for every day, red and white plaid and blue and white. We had a white one, starched and shiny, for Sunday and for company. Our tablecloths were procured from the old peddler who tramped all over the countryside with the huge pack on his back. We traded meat or eggs for anything we could use and keep him overnight. His wares consisted of tablecloths, tinware, handkerchiefs, etc. To Roy and I, he was a breath from the big outside world of which we knew very little. He would always sleep in the barn. Our chores in the summer were pulling weeds for the hogs, picking up cobs for the stove, hunting eggs, and filling the wood box with chips and wood. I enjoyed playing house a lot as Mother would let me dress up in her skirts, and as hoops were in vogue those days, I would make mine out of willow branches tying them with string to suit my size.

When Roy started school I had to play alone a lot but I had lots of imaginary friends. When I was four years old Mother let me go to school with Roy. The teacher boarded with us so she said it would be all right for me to go. I was very proud when, madly holding on to Roy's hand, I trudged along with him bumping my little brass toed shoes on every bunch of dirt, as I was not used to wearing shoes. Mother sent my blocks with me. They were square blocks of wood with letters on two sides and animals on the other two sides. The letters were bright red and the pictures of the dog and cat were black. That was the way I learned my A, B, and C's. I didn't like the first day of school, so on the way home I hid my blocks under a culvert, Roy solemnly promising not to tell on me. As far as I was concerned, my education was over.

Arriving home in our little kitchen Mother asked, "Well, dear, how did you like school?"

"I don't like it. I hate to sit still and the boys pull my braids," I replied.

"Where are your blocks? I'll help you make letters after supper," Mother asked.

I hung my head as I stammered, "I lost them."

"She didn't either, she hid them under that little culvert," shouted Roy.

I made a face at him as Mother said, "You two go right back and find them or no supper. Hurry!" Roy grabbed my arm roughly and dragged me along. I just spat on him but went along.

By the end of the week, I liked school better. I played ante-over, whip cracker, drop the handkerchief and old witch. Across from the schoolhouse was a thick hazel brush and the girls and boys would race out there at noon to gather sheep sorrel and wild onions for our lunch. Mother always sent hard-boiled eggs to school with us and we would crack them on our head so they would peel easily. That term we caught a nice batch of lice and Mother had to wash and comb (with a fine comb) every night with kerosene on the comb.

One chilly morning Roy suggested we visit the traps on our way to school. He and Father kept several traps set a short distance from the road about halfway to school. We went down to the first trap along the little creek and sure enough, a small animal was tugging away at the chain. We approached cautiously and the little fellow was a skunk and he charged! We smelt to high heaven and the teacher sent us home on double quick. Mother, as soon as she got a whiff, made us go to the barn and strip to the skin. She buried our clothes for a day or two before she washed them. Poor Mother, she had plenty of annoyances those days. Then one night we were awakened and hurriedly sent to the neighbor's. Father said to be good children and told us hurry from school the next night and maybe I would have a little sister or brother to hold. I ran most of the way home the next night not waiting for the other children. But when I rushed into the house, Father took me into the bedroom. There was Mother with a red-faced baby beside her. She said I would have to wait a day or two before I could hold him, so every night I would rush home. In a few days, Father placed me in the big red rocker and placed Ray, my new brother, in my arms. I kicked and squalled when Father took him up and placed him back beside Mother. From then on I hurried home just to get to hold him. I watched over him constantly. Sometimes Mother asked the hired girl to hold Ray and Mother would wash the dishes for a change, as it would rest her. Jealously watching the hired girl I would see her slyly pinch Ray when Mother was through with the dishes and make Ray cry so that Mother would have to take him. I saw her pinch him and I rushed into the kitchen and grabbed the butcher knife and would have carved her, I guess, if Mother had not grabbed me. "What do you mean, you bad girl?" Sobbing, I screamed, "I saw her pinch Ray and she made him cry." Mother shoved me into the bedroom and I heard her scolding the girl. From that day on, that hired girl and I were enemies and I would get a good rap when I stuck my finger in the cake batter.

That winter Mother took Roy and me to visit her folks in Canada, and young as I was, it is still very vivid with me. The busy railroad station in Chicago, the ferry crossing from Detroit to Canada, cars being put on the ferry and being ferried across. Then the beautiful home of Grandfather, Cutter rides with bells jingling, and big snow houses big enough to play in. Mother had been reared in a lovely old brick home. I have often wondered many times since how she stood the little bleak house out on the Iowa prairie. Her tasks were always heavy. She always boarded the teacher and had a hired man underfoot to cook for and in those days to wash for too. Milking, raising chicken, taking care of a big garden, helping with the haying and harvest, and we children to take care of. She made all our underwear from bolts of heavy cotton flannel. Also knit all our stockings, mittens, leggings, wristlets, Roy's suits and all of Father's everyday pants out of gray jeans. She dried all our fruits, corn, pumpkins, herbs and made her own soap. She seemed to spend the greater part of the night knitting. I remember the old soap barrel back of the house where all waste grease and wood ashes went to "leach". She made both hard and soft soap. She washed for all of us on the washboard, carrying the water from the old well a rod or so away. Sometimes she would melt the snow for the boiler. Clothes had to be boiled those days. Washing was an all day job. The first boiler of water was for the first washboard scrub and the second boiler was to boil the clothes. The next rubbings after being taken from the boiler and two rinses, one the bluing water. Hot starch had to be made, too. And oh, the ironing with two-thirds of the wash being starched. Then the stoves had to be blacked every Saturday with stove blacking and then rubbed until they shone. Mother's hands never really lost their sullied looks, especially her fingernails, as by the time it started to wear off, it was time to sully them again.

As I became older my job was to polish the knives and forks with brick dust. We kept a pan with part of a brick in it and shaved off the brick as needed. During "fly time" we would pull the shades every morning and open the door. All hands had to drop what they were doing and help "shoo" flies with old aprons, towels or what have you toward the door where the flies would rush out in swarms. Mother took old newspapers folded the size of the door, fringed the edges and tacked them to the screen door; the motion would shoo the flies away the fringe moving with the opening of the door. We were all told to rush in and out and not "let the flies in" but by night the flies were all back in again. Not many had screen doors and windows but we would buy mosquito netting at 5¢ per yard and tack on the windows and the screen door frames.

We children looked forward to the threshing time with all the teams, noise and twenty-three or more men milling around (all neighbors exchanged work). Four teams were hitched to the power and went round and round, hour after hour furnishing the power for the thresher. The beaten circle path was our racetrack after the threshers had gone. We rode many a broomstick around this track and the winner was entitled to the loser's cookie or doughnut. We always felt sorry for the poor horses that went round and round like a merry-go-round and never got anywhere. We loved to watch the men throwing the big grain shucks into the maw of the machine and see the golden grain rolling out. While this was going on the outside with the yells of the men, "Get there, – Whoa, – Haw." Mother on the inside of the house, with the neighboring women, was busy with pies, big roasts of meat, fried chicken and mountains of vegetables. There was always the ever-present cole slaw, sliced tomatoes and stacks of homemade bread and great pots of coffee and pitchers of milk fresh from the nice cool cellar.

Roy and I were both given huge boughs of tree limbs from the maple trees and had to stand by the table (they always ate out-of-doors) and keep the flies from taking over. Often one or two would land in the hot cup of coffee and in the big bowls of gravy. Our little arms would ache from the long siege and there was always the "second" table to do it all over again. We would anxiously watch the last piece of chicken disappear from the platter and we would make faces at the back of the man who speared it away. Those days they stayed for supper too. A few would straggle home but usually the whole mob stayed and the owners of the machine would stay the night and be there for breakfast, too.

We always had spelling school at the schoolhouse, or Lyceum, or occasionally a Punch and Judy show by some traveling shyster. We all were so proud of Father as he was always the last person down at the spelling bee, and then to cap it all, he would end by spelling for the benefit of his admirers the word, "Not-la-zo-ma-nix-to-pix-con-tat-zins". He spelled it a syllable at a time pronouncing each one as he went along. They would cheer him and he would retire from the floor with straight shoulders and a flush of pride. Mother was really bored, I think, but we children loved it. Lots of unhappy things, too, occurred on our farm— the year that corn was but 8¢ per bushel and Father burned it in the stoves as fuel. The time his herd of 50 hogs died of cholera when ready for market. The time he stood gazing out on a golden field of wheat and a few moments later watched hail the size of big marbles reduce it to a sodden mass. That was to be tax money and interest on the mortgage. We loved sorghum-making time too. We would help cut and load the cane and take it to a neighbor who had a mill and watched eagerly the turning of our cane into, to us, delicious sorghum. Flies and bugs had to be fished out once in awhile. We always looked forward to the trip to town for our winter supplies— new clothes, shoes with the shiny brass strip across the toes, yarn for stockings and big bolts of cotton flannel for our underwear. How we loved to spread out our arms and hold the skeins of yarns while Mother rolled it into balls. Often she put it across the back of a chair and let us wind the balls. We dreaded putting on our shoes in the fall after going barefoot all summer.

That makes me think how we would try and sneak into bed at night without washing our feet. Father would sometimes bring us a stick of horehound candy or a lump of brown sugar as a reward for washing our feet. We loved the brown sugar—we just used white sugar when company came. On our birthdays' Mother always made us a cake and decorated it with gumdrops and that went for our school picnics, too. Father made the ice cream, always cooking the rich custard and putting it into a pail with a handle and then placed the pails and then patiently turned the inner pail round and round. Ever so often he would lift the lid to see how it was comin' and we youngsters would scrap to see who would lick the spoon.

Baking day was another looked for event as we were always present when Mother took the fresh bread from the oven and we would wait until she cut off both ends of the loaf, the heel and toe, we called it. She would spread this with gobs of yellow butter and I have never tasted anything since to compare with it. Father always tried to bring us something every time he went to town. One day he brought Roy a tiny evergreen and me a rose bush. He immediately set them out. In a few days, Roy decided that we should move the rosebush nearer the house so he just cut it off and replanted the stock. Fifty years later, tears came to my eyes as I saw his evergreen, towering up into the blue sky where, maybe, he is now.

When my brother Ray was two years old, another baby boy arrived, Guy. I loved and tended him as faithfully as I did Ray. Ray was now at the age of walk, talk and balk. We had a bunch of asparagus in our front yard as an ornament (those days we did not know we could eat it) and Ray was always breaking it off or eating the red berries which Mother was always afraid would poison him.

Mother taught us to see beauty everywhere–busy as she was; she would always stop her work to view a beautiful sunset or formations of lovely clouds. She loved the stars and one night she dragged me up from the floor where I had fallen asleep, put on my coat and took me out to the orchard where the trees were ablaze with colored lights green, red, purple, shining like diamonds. Moonlight on the heavy frost made it a fairyland. I thank her always for the lovely memory.

Often she would take me to the North end of the farm, all virgin sod and we would pick wildflowers–tiger lilies, lady slippers and sweet williams. These few acres were always alive with flowers. We would hunt until we would find Jack–in–the–Pulpit, wild strawberries and ink plant. Then in the fall, there was the day for going "nutting." We had but to go a mile or so for worlds of walnuts (black), butternuts, and hazelnuts. Then home and all hands putting the nuts on top of sheds and house roof to dry for later husking off the outer shells. Our hands would be stained for the rest of the winter. Our wildflower retreat was slowly yielding to Father's demand for more crops, and we would drop corn in the space left when Father would lift a shovelful of sod and place it back on the corn. He always had a good crop from this procedure–maybe an acre at a time until the virgin sod was gone and so were our wildflowers.

How we loved the call of the Whip-poor-will, Bobwhite and the Mourning Dove. I heard them once again on this trip I made back there and saw again the "lightning bugs," as Roy and I called them. Roy and I used to catch them and put them into bottles until Mother would make us turn them loose. They were beautiful; these moving specks of light as they flew just at twilight time. How I have missed all of this–the dear, dead past. This would not sound interesting to the children of today, but you see, our days were full of these simple ways of life. It is so restful to go from this hustle and bustle to the dear old farmlands; in the bluestem pastures there is always brooding peace and a calm and serene beauty, a soothing benediction ever ready for those who are spiritually attuned to accept it.

We had our humorous times too, like when we heard the hired girl upstairs yelling frantically for Mother. Father was first to reach her room and he nearly exploded with laughter as he met all of us at the head of the stairs. It seems that Martha, the girl, had been to a circus several days before and now was trying an acrobatic feat of getting both feet behind her neck and did get one leg up, but was unable to extricate herself. Mother and Father helped her back to her normal self. School was not in session, so we youngsters could not spread the news.

There was always, in those days, the "summer kitchen" that everyone had back then. The summers were so hot and with the big cook stove always on the job, the house would be unbearable to sleep in. The first sign of summer's approach would be Mother hustling about in the outside summer kitchen built a few feet away from the main house. Surplus junk would take its usual pilgrimage to the woodshed and barn, then after supper when the cookstove had cooled off, the men about would take down the pipe and clean it good and remove the stove, the black monster, out to the summer kitchen, set it up again so everything would be in order for the "before daylight" breakfast. Mother would be engineering the feat with a kerosene lamp in her hand, sometimes tipped dangerously as she engineered the pipe connecting.

Then there was the goose feather picking time when each goose was caught and held between Mother's knees. They would try to fight and squawk while she relentlessly robbed them of their plumage. Mother was always making a new feather bed. Speaking of beds, after threshing time, the straw ticks were emptied of the old straw and we would carry the clean ticks to the straw stack and fill them with the new fresh straw and pack them until they looked like balloons. The old slat beds then received the straw ticks and then over them was placed the fluffy feather ticks. What a bed! We children liked the first few nights on those beds, so high that we had to climb up on the kitchen chairs to get into them.

In house cleaning time, the old rag carpet went through the same treatment. We youngsters pulled all the tacks, which were a few inches apart and then the carpet was put on the clothesline and for several days we took turns beating the dust out of it. The old chewed up straw was removed from the floor and new straw piled on several inches thick. Then down on this went the carpet again, the men stretching it while Mother tacked it down again. Then we would turn somersaults on it till Mother drove us out with the broom. Later mechanical carpet stretchers could be had. Later the straw gave way to old newspapers. In our living room was always the center table with the big Bible and the picture album and a seashell or two that would moan when placed to the ear. Visitors were always entertained by looking through the family album viewing with comments on the dress and customs of the hairstyles. Always on the wall, there was a bunch of peacock feathers and a bunch of seaweed tied with a fancy ribbon. Over the chair backs there were antimacassars, and in one corner would be the easel with a large picture of one of the family in a huge gold frame, and draped over one corner would be a large embroidered "throw" the size of a bath towel. An organ most always had its place in the sitting room, too, as well as a horsehair sofa and chairs and a footstool or two.

The guest bedroom had its bowl and pitcher and the stand or commode to keep it on. Back of the bowl and pitcher would be a "splasher," another piece of embroidered linen and under the bed was the "chamber," usually with a crocheted cover on the lid to muffle the sound of an emergency. There were the pillow shams, starched stiff, to spread over the pillows through the day. Usually, angel heads and wings were outlined on each sham or the words "Sleep Gently." We felt real proud when we could afford a commode for our washbowl and pitcher. It had a rail on the back, too, for our nice "splasher" and a door for the chamber, much better than under the bed. Grandma crocheted a nice cover for the top to eliminate those "embarrassing moments," she said.

Father decided to vaccinate us. He had something in a bottle from the doctor and each of us took turns in having our arms scratched with his little penknife (he did plunge it into hot water before the scratch act) and then applied the stuff in the bottle. My arm was swollen to nearly twice its size and I remember I was pretty sick for a few days. I still have the tiny white scar on my arm. Many mothers, at a much later date, had their daughters vaccinated in places they wrongfully thought would never show. Some of the marks can be seen now on the beaches.

Grandmother would not be vaccinated. She was as boring as an endless freight train. She sat by the stove day in and day out quoting scripture, with a little black shawl over her shoulders and a black lace cap. When we were naughty, we had to listen to her reading until we were too tired to stand. Later after she had me read it all through I asked her, "He went in unto her and she conceived—" but before I finished my quiz, I received a nice slap for my inquiry. I never saw her help Mother with the dishes, pare any vegetables, dust or mend and now when I look back she was at that time only 69 years of age.

Poor Mother would sit up nights during corn husking time to mend gloves and make fresh finger "cots" for the coming day. She made them for the index finger where the husking peg wore through. Each had a string sewed on to tie them to the wrist. As young as Roy and I were, we were awakened before daylight, ate our heavy breakfast of fried potatoes, hot biscuits, ham and eggs and mush, jump on those cold wagons before it was really daylight and husk what was then called the "down row" which was crushed down by the wagon passing over it. We would husk that row and throw in the high wagon. That was one time when we were glad when the winter term of school started, to get out of cornhusking. But Saturday we were on the job again. Poor tired little backs! But there was always the hot dinner awaiting us; steamed cornbread, fried pork and gravy, potatoes baked and fluffy, and baked beans ending with a suet pudding or mince pie—not so bad. No juvenile delinquency then. Nostalgically, I go back again and again in my dreams. Where have the lovely childhood days gone?

When Roy was twelve and I was ten, we moved to our little town and lived in a little rented house. It was all so different and for the first time we were really unhappy.

We missed our animal friends and the wildlife that was all around us, even to the big wolfhounds of our neighbor, who in the winter was hunting timber wolves, and the baying of the hounds was music to us. Grandpa moved to town with us, as Grandma had died the year before. He was so huge that when he sat down, he had to hold a good portion of himself in his lap. His eyebrows made an unbroken road across his face, sinking into a valley on his nose, and he had the tiredest eyes of anyone in the world. He would let me comb his hair an hour at a time with his fine-tooth comb. He always carried an ear spoon in his wallet and I liked to watch him at his daily chore of digging out his ears, meanwhile humming, "Yankee Doodle." Grandpa was immaculate about his person and we children loved him. He was fun while Grandma was always dictatorial and tiresome but we were taught to give them both our love and respect. Grandpa didn't like town any more than the rest of us and he missed Grandma, too. I think Mother enjoyed being the one woman in the house. She was always kind to Grandma but she did resent the "peddlin and the medlin" that she engaged in between the relatives.

School was a change for Roy and me, and was really hard too. Ray and Guy were more content than the rest of us but, of course, they were still babies and one place was as good as another. More and more of my time at home was taken up with them as they always wanted to be with me as soon as I came from school. I was glad to get home to them, too. The children at school did not mean to be cruel (and children can be terribly cruel) but to them we were "hicks" from the country, but in a short time they accepted us as one of them and we were better satisfied.

We lived at the foot of a hill, and up on the hill lived an old lady alone, who was very cross and stingy. Her daughter's husband kept a grocery store and she said he had taken most of her money to start his store and would not give it back to her. In those days, big baskets of eggs were on benches along the sidewalk in front of the stores for sale with other farm produce. Mrs. Shaw, the old lady, took a fiendish pleasure in walking up and down the street in front of his store and poking her cane into the baskets of eggs, breaking them. They were about ten cents a dozen. I liked to visit with her and hear her stories of the early days of Iowa, ten or fifteen years before we came to Iowa. She always had a fence post or broken tree burning in her fat bellied stove. One end rested on a chair while the other end burned in the stove with the door wide open. She had an old tub to catch the sparks and a bucket of water to douse if the floor would catch fire; She would keep pushing the log into the stove until it was all burned up.

Later, we bought her house and were quite proud of the five rooms and of being "hill folks." In the cellar was a cave for tornadoes and at every dangerous looking cloud, Mother would herd us into the cellar and then into that hole or cave until the storm was over. We there bought our first store carpet, a sleazy affair with huge autumn leaves woven through it. To us, it was a pure Persian. We had a new felt scarf for our center table with yellow velvet strips cat stitched across each end with green and yellow ribbon running through slits above that. We were so proud of our "sitting room." Mother bought some new clothes for herself and us children. I remember one of her dresses was made with an overskirt which had a series of puffs made over her hips and the big bustle. She would stand for hours, it seemed to us, when she was fitted by the dressmaker to get those puffs just right.

We children were sent to Sunday School and Mother sang in the choir. The church had a small library and

I simply ate up those stories; "Little Women," "Little Men," " Jo's Boat," "Christie's Xmas," naming a few. I think I went to Sunday School just to bring home the books, for the characters in those books were very real folks to me, my friends and chums.

Mother took in day boarders, including some from the Teachers Institute, she would always have two teachers to house and board. That was when I decided to be a teacher, so I could go to the Institute and have good food to eat. Then, too, I loved my eighth grade teacher with dog-like devotion and I wanted to be like her. I see her yet with her hair combed in a double pompadour and the long white starched apron she always wore. I cried my heart out when I was promoted to the ninth grade (upstairs). Forty years later, I again saw her in Long Beach, California and still loved her. I had lots of escapades in school. My chum and I decided to wear bustles to school (10th Grade) so we borrowed our mother's bustles under our short dresses and marched into the schoolroom. We did not realize that our dresses were shortened in the back and that our panties were showing. There was an uproar of laughter and we were immediately sent home. We tried doing our hair up in a Physche Knot, then in style for adults, so to make it protrude farther out from the head, we stuck a pencil in it as an ornament. Again, we were sent home. The school installed a furnace, so we tried to slide down the coal chute and emerged blackened and were discharged. Then we would ask to leave the room and take some one's sled and try steering down the long hill by ourselves, forgetting to return to the schoolroom. Mother and teacher both were at their wit's end trying to solve a way to cure us of our mad capers. But I managed to be promoted, so I did not worry too much.

Things were getting a bit hard for Mother, too, for Father was not much of a success in town as a provider.

He knew farming as it was practiced in those days. He bought out a livery stable and that was not paying too well. Mother still kept boarders and managed in some way to keep we children in school and well fed and well dressed.

Roy had taken a job that he was very proud of. Nearly all the town folk kept a cow and Roy took on the responsibility of rounding up eight cows and taking them to the "commons" adjoining the town, herding them, and bringing them back at night to be milked at their respective homes. His poor little legs would ache from trying to keep them together and getting them in their proper yards at night. It was hard to keep the herd together.

So, the days of childhood sped by. A day is an odd sort of unit. It begins, flows like a tiny rivulet toward eternity and ends as we fall asleep. No day can ever be like any other day. We can, and do, store more precious moments away in memory but nothing ever repeats itself. And so, when I awake each morning, I have learned to think of the day ahead as a new world to adventure in. I want my days to be filled with living and I think they were, especially in my later years.

The Central House

Our next move was to the town hotel, called the Central House. My father looked forward to being the landlord of a country hotel with joy and a bit of anticipation. He thought money would simply roll in. Mother, for awhile, was to do the cooking herself. It was not a desirable life for a family of children. I was fourteen at the time, Roy was sixteen, and Ray and Guy were little boys. Of course, grandfather went with us. Today the little country hotel is teetering on the brink of oblivion. The trailer, motor courts, tourist homes, and the miracle of motoring have all played their part in its undoing. In retrospect, these havens seemed notable contributions to community content.

To we children, in our formative days, in what then appeared to be an exciting flurry of travel, strange faces and constant change, the country hotel was the hub of the village. Most of the news from the outside radiated from there. From the city, drum town slickers acquired their sartorial stick. It was where the troupers stopped when they came with their tricks of illusion, soubrettes, villains and handsome heroes. The hotel office was where the men of the town gathered when night came on. It was where the mighty questions of the day were settled, where the scandals of the town were aired and where men argued valiantly and often in apoplectic rage over the "goings on in Washington." Country hotel offices were cut to a familiar fashion or pattern, rather. There was the semi-circular reception desk with the open register where pens spiked in a raw potato or cup of birdshot. Alongside was the cigar case. Back of them the big iron safe, the key rack and clock whose face heralded the miracles of some medical bitters. The inevitable roller towels over the washbasin, the boarders whirling them around to find a dry clean place to wipe their hands. Centering the room, the pot-bellied stove festooned with its yawning boxes of sand that served as cuspidors. On the side was the writing desk with half a dozen chairs and in the corner a high shoeshine chair, operated by the combination porter, bellboy and houseman, all in one. On a table, a row of well cleaned and filled kerosene lamps all ready to light the guest to his room. Some of the bowls had strips of red flannel soaked with the kerosene to add to their attractiveness.

The dining room led off the office through swing doors and there was a rack of hats at the entrance—no snide hat checking in those days. There was the drummer's table distinguished by a bowl of city oranges and bananas, and from the ceiling hung an enormous and smelly kerosene lamp.

Waitresses were rather "flip" from our town and usually they were talked about by wagging tongues of old ladies—some more of the "meddlin' and peddlin." Sometimes they married into good families and made splendid wives but were rarely accepted into the social realm.

The general run of country hotels was from $1.00 to $2.00 per day and that included a room and three meals. And what meals! At breakfast, for instance, the aproned waitress sing-songed over your shoulder, "Bacon and eggs, fried chicken, steak with onions, sausage and griddle cakes, pork chops with apple rings and spare ribs." With the entrée came a variety of tempting doo-dads such as fried mush, hominy grits and buttered beets served in birdcage dishes, called side dishes. All the milk and coffee you could drink and no sniffs at requests for second helpings. Many hotels were so comfortable and homelike; they won for the village the sobriquet of "Sunday town." Ours was like that. Drummers came Saturday nights and stayed until Monday and thus the hotel office on Saturday night was awash with a thrilling cosmopolitanism. All the chairs were occupied and the locals loafed about bug-eyed with the sudden rub with the outside world and the citified yarn spinning. In one corner, a pitch, seven-up, or cribbage game and the room was literally opalescent with cigar and pipe smoke.

The town drunk, Leggy, often wandered in and would weave about in an alcoholic blur until led out. Leggy realized he was never welcome and was always dog-like in humility. There was a real heartiness though about the crowd in the hotel office. Their ribaldry and the raw flavor of the barnyard but somehow, it was wholesome in contrast to the psychopathic pap of today. Many were pipe smokers and tobacco chewers with a wardrobe of but two suits—one for work and one for "nice." But they were substantial folk with respect for law and the rights of man and the Constitution. God-fearing described them. Sunday mornings in seasonable weather, the chairs were placed at the curb and the office moved out to watch the town go by to the post office and to church. The farm boys would come in on horseback in their Sunday suits and rack their mounts to the hitch rack, across the street, and gawk at the girls and city folks. Giddy girls would flounce by affecting indifference, but half a block away, stop at some window and glance back expectantly. How prosaic it all is now to recall and yet how tremendous for all of us.

We were all so happy in this new environment except poor Mother. She was busy every minute, it seemed. Every day was different. Some days we would have a show troupe of five to eight people and to me they were something from another world with their make-believe lives. Of course, we were given free tickets and no girl ever had more friends at these times than I—all fishing for free tickets or a chance to flirt with the show folks.

The medicine shows were welcome, too. We had the old Kickapoo Indian medicine show with three real Indians, the first real Indians we children had ever seen. I was afraid of them, too, with their headdress of feathers and silent ways. One day coming in from the street, Yellow Dog, jumped from behind a door with an unearthly yell;

I just proceeded to faint! He knew I was afraid of him and wanted to give me a good scare. Their old boss, The Doctor, barked his wares from the stage or his wagon according to the weather and people flocked to him after the show to buy the stuff....good for everything.

Then there was always the night oyster suppers for the dancers in the old opera house a few doors away. This was always a midnight affair and if Father was out, Mother would send me to the hall to announce the supper was ready and this one night, I was the only one available, so hesitantly, she sent me. I was never allowed to dance but loved it and she cautioned me just to go to the door and call someone to announce it and hurry back. I made the door okay, but one of our boarders spied me (he was a bit "gone" on me), grabbed me by the arm and said, "Come waltz this one out." I tried to tell him that Mother was checking on me but he dragged me in, I was rather willing, I guess, too. I was soon in the clouds, dancing to my heart's content but was suddenly interrupted when Father appeared at the door and said Mother was frantic. Father understood and I know he wanted me to stay but we both knew better. Yes, I was certainly in the doghouse that night! I remember what a glorious night it was—a few particles of snow were coming down like samples, the night as quiet as a kitten on cotton, the stars were leaning against the sky, glittering with a touch of tomorrow. You see, I was experiencing my first thrill of being loved (as I thought).

Mother was too busy right then to say much and I hoped, in the rush and excitement of the couples trying to reach the tables first, she might forget entirely. While we were clearing away the supper, Father, who was helping reset the tables for breakfast, said to Mother, "We can just hope, Mother, that we will live long enough to be as big a nuisance to our children as they are now to us." But it didn't work, for she took me to task good and plenty.

Then one day, coming home from school, I was overjoyed to find a new Camp piano in our front parlor. Father had bought it from a piano salesman who always put up with us. Mother didn't approve and quickly informed us, as Roy was the oldest, he would have the first lessons. I was so disappointed but Roy didn't last long, only a few lessons. Someone had shown him how to play, "Peter, Peter Pumpkin," with his two front fingers and he thumped that out hour after hour but would not practice his lessons. Even Mother was disgusted and then my lessons started. My teacher was blind and she needed the money so Mother had her come once a week at $2.54 a lesson. I loved to practice and later I had a much better teacher. The piano has been a source of pleasure to me always.

Roy left school in his 16th year and became an apprentice in a blacksmith shop. He loved tools and machinery and one day when on the program in English for a speech, he simply bowed to the room, stuttered and stammered, not remembering a word of his speech, bolted from the room and nothing could induce him to go back.

I rather liked my school work, staggering through Caesar with his "All Gaul is divided into three parts," and etc. Slowly crawling through geometry and algebra with its unknown quantity was not the only unknown quantity in my last year of High School – all but my English Literature. I loved every word of it. Our class played each Shakespearean play we studied and although I wasn't chosen Portia in Merchant of Venice, I thought I was the world's greatest actress in the part of Jessica and I fairly adored the moonlight scene. The world lost a fine potential actress when I decided to teach a country school!

The big day, Graduation Day, came at last. The day when I thought that all my responsibilities would be over. I had the class prophecy as my subject (all the wonderful future I had pictured for all of my classmates, we were all girls).

All of us that night had throats as tight as tourniquets. Our proud families were all there, of course. Each one of us had our address prepared and we all glued our eyes to the ceiling, chandelier the target, in the very dome of the church and sing-songed our poor little talks to the end. My dress was my mother's wedding dress, white satin, made over for the occasion, and I guess I was pretty "fetching" in it, as the banker's son met me at the door and wanted to walk me home, about three blocks. He gallantly carried my flowers, baskets and bouquets, while I clung desperately to my diploma, the passport to my big dreams. I was so happy. I remember the trees were top-heavy with bird buds, the sequined skies were all aglitter and hesitant moonlight speckled the sidewalk filtering through the high haze and I remember the courthouse clock scissoring towards eleven o'clock. I was treading air but I was shy and self-conscious too, remembering the banker's son was my escort. How innocent and childish can one get?

CHAPTER III

Finding My Way

(1894 On-ward)

◆

There wasn't much for girls to do those days, —teaching, nursing, clerking in a store, college or office work which was frowned upon, being cooped up all day in an office with a Man! That was the verdict of most of all the old "biddies" around town. So I chose teaching. How I dreaded taking the examination to get a certificate to teach. Our county superintendent was the "bogey man" for we girls who had decided upon teaching and we were all scared stiff. I was two days writing, chewing my pencil and trying to think of the answers. I was restless and worried for ten days waiting to get the returns from the Superintendent. And then one day it was in the mail. There it was—that bit of paper that said I could teach. Pretty good grades, too!

Now then for a school to teach. Teachers were pretty plentiful as I found out trudging from one township to another. I walked and rode in a two-wheeled cart hitched to our old Dolly horse through wind, rain and dust, contacting Directors of these little schools. They were puffed up like a bubble, being the big man of the district. Most of them hired their teachers for fall (we had three terms then) spring three months, fall two months, and winter four months, and they just hired the teachers for a term at a time. Most of them thought I was too young—seventeen. At last, my best friend's father, who was our County Treasurer, referred me to a friend of his who was a director and advised me to see him at once as he had spoken to him about me and had recommended me. This school was fourteen miles away, a long distance those days, but I hitched up old Dolly to the two-wheeled cart and started out. I didn't get there until noon. Mr. Lambert, the director, looked me over and then with a twinkle in his old German eyes said, "Did I understand that you wanted to attend our school or was it to teach?" I gave him a sneering smile and in a few words told him I was there to teach. He chuckled but I left with a signed contract to teach two months at $25 a month and they would board me for $1.50 per week. I headed homeward like a homing pigeon.

The sky was brushed red with the sun like ostrich feathers on fire and the great elms along the road stood apart and listened as I sang, "In the Shade of the Old Apple Tree", "Two Little Girls in Blue" and ending with "Down Went McGinty," as Dolly jogged along towards oats and rest. I had started on my road to fame. My family was jubilant at my success. After my board was paid, the rest would be "velvet" as there was no way to spend money way out there. I rehearsed my first day over and over again, the way I would open school, etc. I contacted an old teacher and she gladly gave me the help I needed. Packing my trunk and my treasured book, I started out to my first school and first job, on top of the world. How proud when I had gotten through my first day with flying colors dead sure of myself.

The children were all dears. There were sixteen of them. Of course, I had all grades from beginners to eighth grade. All had slates with those long slate pencils, the tops wrapped with red, white and blue papers. All were experts, spitting on their slates and wiping it off with one swoop of the rag. I soon installed wet sponges. Twice a day two youngsters asked to go after a pail of drinking water. They had about one-eighth of a mile to go for well water and about one half of it would be sloshed out by the time they got back to school. The older ones always went to draw the well water with buckets, as they were strong enough to draw it and carry it back. Then the bucket was passed from seat to seat, all drinking from the one long handled dipper. Sanitation? Not in the dictionary, my dear. At noon, teachers went out to play too—ante-over, crack the whip and drop the handkerchief. That fall was beautiful, soft as summer at midday, so warm and dreamy that one tends to believe that it will last forever. Comes the blue dusk, edged with coolness and a silver knife seems to slice away the heat.

I was a bit homesick and the longing to see my friends and relatives was quite urgent at times. I loved my work and the children with their funny little ways. They brought me fruit and flowers they had picked along the roadside and sometimes a bunch of radishes or green onions. The last day of school was always an event in country schools. A little program would be arranged, picture cards given and a picnic. When the fond mothers and sometimes the fathers would come with huge baskets of good things to eat and oodles of ice cream which was a real treat. It was about the only amusement for them outside of Fourth of July and the County Fair in the fall.

After a full feed and everybody happy. Fourth of July was a big day for country folk those days. Again the big baskets would be packed in the back of the wagons or buggies and neighbors met and joined on the green under a tree at noon for their dinner. Tablecloths were spread on the grass and all hands circled on knees or buttocks. It was a happy time for all. Large families all came in the farm wagon if Father was lucky in borrowing extra spring seats from some bachelor or from someone that could not go to these celebrations. The children filled up on pink lemonade at the stands for 5 cents a glass and then flocked to the merry-go-round at 5 cents per ride. There was always the balloon ascension that was a great attraction watching the great bag filled with air then the thrilling moment when it took off—eager eyes watching and then a breathless cry as the man jumped from the parachute. Then the wagons were loaded again for the home trip. Baskets now packed with the reproach of dirty dishes. Children were tired but contented and quiet as a thermometer going up. It was dark before the tired horses turned into the old wire gate. Fireflies were glimmering their lanterns in the meadows as grey cotton clouds stretched across the moon. So the day ended.

Going back to the little school—lots of interesting things happened in those little institutions. Another experience during my first term of teaching was a tornado. All schools were required to have storm caves and teachers were instructed to take all the children to the cave if a threatening storm came in sight. When the sky grows green and the air smells funny, we would grab up the little ones, first graders, and the others were trained to follow, help with the little tots and get in the cave pronto. Some supplies are also kept in the cave in case something might happen that we could not get out for a spell after the storm was over. Something might or could fall on the door of the cave. After a storm, the air is as clear as a glass bell and the world has a freshness that makes one feel that it had just been created that very day. I had a few music students, too, and after school was out for the day I would go home with the child taking lessons from me, give the lesson for 25 cents an hour and then afterwards walk to my boarding house or one of the family would take me back after they milked the cattle. Usually, I had a wonderful supper before leaving.

These little schools all used the now famous McGuffey Readers and Ray's Arithmetic. No reader has ever taken their place in the hearts of America. I remember so clearly the poem entitled, "We Are Seven." Nothing more stirring and beautiful was ever written. I had many funny experiences during my teaching days. At one school, I was forced to board with the dirtiest housekeeper in the district. Chickens ran in and out of the kitchen to their heart's content(no screen doors), cats and dogs, too. One huge dog always sat by his master and would watch his chance to grab a big slab of meat from his plate. The man would never stop talking and when he missed his meat, he would just fork another slab and slam it on top of the place where the dog had fetched his other slab. So I always took food in a telescope suitcase to eat after I was supposed to be in bed. You can't lock a telescope suitcase so one night my landlady took me to task for bringing food from home. I just told her that I wanted to lunch in the night. So it went. I taught twelve of these terms of school and then decided I was not getting very far along teaching a country school and decided to take a business course, so after the fall corn husking, I decided on the Dixon College in Dixon, Illinois.

Returning to the cornfields of Iowa, many were over 100 acres in size, so large that one could easily get lost in them, which Roy and I did one time when we were small.

We followed some little pigs that seemed lost and when we tried to corral them, they took for the cornfield. In no time we lost them, even their grunts, and in a short time we were hopelessly lost, too. "I think we'd better follow just one row and it will have to end someplace and we can see where we are," said Roy, which was a very wise thing to do and so we trudged on and on stumbling over cockle burrs and a few sandburrs stuck to our clothes. Petals of wild sunflowers dropped to the ground like tired butterflies and fat bumblebees blundered against the broad faces of the sunflowers, too. Fat caterpillars tufted like toothbrushes inching along the stalks of the sunflowers. The corn, too, showed through like teeth in a sudden yellow grin. These things I still remember, frightened as I was. Soon a fence came in sight; we were at the end of the field, but which end? Then I saw smoke swirling out of a chimney like lover's fingers and I knew it was HOME. After fifty years of being lost, not in a cornfield, but out in a modern world, peering through the yesteryears is like looking through the wire fence—I see again the welcome smoke.

It is easy to become unreasonably nostalgic about the old things and our childhood days. The old prices of things come back to me, too, wishing them back again. I remember the one-horse meat wagon that always came to our home once a week, sometimes twice, round steak, 10 cents per lb., saddle of lamb, 25 cents, veal, 10 cents, and porterhouse steak, 20 cents. Beef was a treat, for we always had so much pork, home butchered and cured. Beef was a treat along with oranges, horehound candy, and gumdrops.

I think of the wintertime storytelling around a wood burning stove, of sleigh rides in the cold biting air and the never-to-be-forgotten music of sleigh bells, of the coasting down the long hill that went right through the main street of our town to the river. Fifteen or more could ride on those sleds sitting with legs sprawled out so as not to touch the ground as we sped down the hill. Then the long walk back pulling the heavy bob just to ride down again.

Riding bobs just made me think of our old train, Betsy Ann, that came in once a day at 4 o'clock. It was a treat when we could meet the train and view the ten or twelve people who might come in on it. The last stop before it came to our town was 5 miles away, a little town dubbed, Monteith. My chum, May, had never ridden on a train, so we saved our pennies from Sunday School and when we had 11 cents we walked to Monteith and excitedly waited for the 4 o'clock train to ride back to our town. How proudly we stepped off with the other passengers. We had never been missed from our homes. Imagine youngsters of today getting a thrill out of a stunt like that.

So life in our little town went on with the same old faces, same old pleasures and looking back I can see how free and happy we really were. The only new people who ever came to our town was maybe a new professor, new minister, occasionally, but always twice a year was the new "trimmer," who came to the millinery shop to trim our hats. Those days we selected our hats unadorned and would pick out the ribbon, flowers, stuffed bird, fruit, or feathers and then the trimmer arranged this on our hats and made them a thing of beauty, or so we thought. The price was all the way from $1.50 to $3.00. We were shocked one spring when the banker's wife paid $5.00 for a hat, the only one in the shop. After I had taken the business course in Dixon College of which I will tell you later, I took the position as bookkeeper and buyer for ladies shoes, dry goods and ready to wear goods. I was pretty proud, as it was the largest general store in the town that gave me this position. My hours were long, from 7 AM. to 9 PM. and 10 PM. depending if there were late shoppers. I scarcely ever had the cash "made up" and safe locked before 9:30 PM. At invoice time we would stay as late as 2 AM. or 3 AM., eating bologna and crackers or a few cookies for our midnight snack, as there were no places open to eat at that time. I loved the store and the handling of money. Twice a year, I went to "market" to buy; to Chicago, Omaha, and St. Louis. This was a wonderful experience for me and I felt very important. I remember coming back from a buying trip one time on the train, Betsy Ann, and when I came to our little depot, the band was there and the platform full of people and I wondered if I was the one they were greeting. There were but three passengers that day, a boy, and a man who slept most of the way with his hat pulled down over his face and myself. The man aroused when we reached the depot and the mayor and our banker rushed in and shook his hand and the band started up. He was William Jennings Bryan, coming there to make a speech. My tail feathers dropped! I was in that store until it sold, over seven years. I had wonderful contacts and lots of experiences while there that would make a book of its own.

I knew all the country folk for miles around, not only from teaching among them, but contacting them in the store made them all seem like one big family. We all loved and shared all the "goings on" in our community— weddings, funerals, good times and hard times. There were no income taxes, no permits to buy, no licenses for anything. We were as free as the air itself. We just saved for our taxes which were very small and worked out our road tax and that was it. Hunt and fish anywhere, ride as fast or as slow as you wished and no beggars at the door every hour or so for a "benefit."

Homesteading in North Dakota

After I left the store, I worked in a law office working with abstracts, and other stores, but I was restless and longed to own something of my very own. Land and farms still were my first love and at that time claims were still to be had in North Dakota and a friend of mine, Grace Sutton, and myself decided to go to North Dakota to teach and hold down a claim. We could get $50 per month teaching. Those days you could file on 160 acres and prove up in five years or after a year or so, pay $1.25 an acre and it was yours. We bid our friends adieu and started for what we thought were the "wilds." Dakota! Two states but one land. Dakota means "being friendly" or "allies." It was a never-to-be-forgotten trip—exciting journey through this vast frightening, often incredibly beautiful land. Dakota, the home of the unearthly Badlands, a region barren of everything but awesome beauty. On its fringe, it was slightly tamed by ranchland but it was on to North Dakota, the home of killing blizzards and bitter cold often below 45° and more, that we were going to. Here and there a town lost in the immensity of the land. It is treeless and a country marked by lonely buttes and vision races out a hundred miles or more in every direction and often you see mirages of towns and lakes hundreds of miles away. Distances constantly deceive. It was a horse country and we girls were soon riding the broncos to school and back, the only two schools in the township.

We made headquarters at the Bar D cattle ranch, forty miles from town. The ranch owner was glad to board us, furnish the mounts to go to our schools, for they needed teachers badly. We soon filed on 160 acres each not too far from his ranch. Quite a few men from St. Paul and Minneapolis were there on claims and they were required to stay a night or two every six months, they were very kind to help Grace and I build our little sod houses, a Government requirement and dig us a shallow well even if there was no water in it. We had "Monkey Ward" stoves and a few pieces of rough furniture. We were required to stay a night or two every six months as I recall now, to establish residence. Our claims were not very far apart. Often, though we stayed alone when it was required to spend a night or so in our shacks. One night I heard a tapping on my window and was scared out of my wits. As it periodically continued, I thought I had better find out just who or what it was. I cautiously crept across the floor until I was under the window and lifting the paper curtain, I saw a small bird pecking on the window. A high lonesome moon tilted against the sky like a half slice of lemon had attracted his attention to the outside and he wanted out. With a sigh of relief, I shot back to my bed greatly relieved but I could not sleep again and was glad when the first flaming flashes of dawn reflected pinkly on my wall. We would tether our ponies on a long rope near the cabin to graze on the tall grass all around us grass that we felt friendly toward for the lack of flowers and shrubs. It always seemed to arouse itself at the sheerest whisper of wind, which was always music to us, so shut away from the world.

One night when Grace stayed with me, we tethered our ponies out as usual. We heard a loud whinnying and stamping of hoofs and hurried out to see what was wrong but we were too late. The horses, driven nearly crazy by the swarms of mosquitoes that came buzzing in at dusk, broke their ropes and tails were fast disappearing over the tall grass. We were afoot and quite a long walk to anywhere but we knew there was no use to chase them and hoped they would go to the ranch and the cowboys would round them up and come to our assistance. So they did, and while we were eating our breakfast, a welcome sound seemed to rip through the fabric of silence and the familiar "Yip, Yipee, Yip," met our ears and there were the boys with our mosquito bitten broncos right at our door. We gave them a hearty welcome and glanced at our fuel bag to see if we had enough left for a fire to make them more coffee. Our fuel was the buffalo chips we would pick up and put in a gunnysack. It made an excellent fire and we tried to keep a full sack by our stoves all of the time. We had to go only a short distance to pick it up. We would go different directions dragging our sacks and pick up the chips like our lives depended on it. There was a world of it as this had been a grazing country for years and years. We could also pick up lots of buffalo horns on our claims especially near the buffalo "wallows," which were depressions in the earth where the buffaloes had congregated and stood. There were a lot of small rocks laid in perfect circles in different spots. We were told that they were placed around the Indian wigwams when they used to camp there. It weighted the wigwams down.

Dancing was the main amusement there in the Dakota land, for these prairie folk. They would come 25 to 30 miles to these dances. We danced all night and no one dared to find their way home as there were no roads but just trails and it was so easy to turn off on the wrong one as they forked in so many directions on those big expanses. Not even a fence to guide one. Old folks, young folks, children and babies all came. The babies were all laid out on a bed, the big stove moved out to the kitchen where two sets could be danced. By morning the babies were crying for attention, most of them soaked and, yes, the bed soaked, too. What a gathering! At midnight we had huge pots of coffee passed around and thick homemade bread beef sandwiches, pie and cake. Women of the neighborhood, a radius of 25 or 30 miles, would bring the pie and cake and other goodies. Jolly times, you bet. Everything was free and we did not know nor care if our hair was done in the latest style or our clothes either. Our mail was relayed once a week and sometimes it would be a month before we could get it owing to the weather. Often in the winter, we would have as low as forty–five degrees below or colder. And blizzards there, were really blizzards!

One night at the Bar D, we had to get supper down to the corrals where the owner was staying with his herd to keep them on the move and not pile up. There was a strong wire stretched from the house to the corrals and we had to hold on to the wire with one hand and with food in the other feel our way to the corrals. We did not dare let go of the wire for we could be lost in a few moments. This one particular night, the snow was so dense, we could not even see the lighted lanterns strung along the wire.

Our schools were provided with lots of lignite coal, the coal room being attached to the school. There was a couch to sleep on, in case the teacher was caught in a storm or in bad weather. If she preferred to stay in the school building. Many days no children would come on account of drifts or bitter cold. There is no place on earth as lonely as an empty school room in a blizzard with the ghostly whispers around the windows ending in a wild shriek as the wind grew in intensity. The prairie fires were another hazard that the lonely teacher in Dakota had to cope with. Plow guards were plowed wide around the schoolhouse and not much grass survived on the playground but when we saw the huge blanket of smoke swooping down on us. Children would be herded inside, windows and doors locked, guarded by the teacher and the older pupils to keep children who might panic and rush out to get home and be lost in the onrushing fire for it traveled at a terrific speed. It would halt at the guards but with a stiff wind, it would jump the school building, as there was nothing for its hungry tongue to lick on the grounds. The schoolhouse would be in darkness when this happened, filled with the wails and screams of the small children. Then later we would venture out to see if our roof was intact for a small spark could be dangerous with everything as dry as a sermon.

Then the mosquitoes. Several times a day when the windows were crawling with them, the teacher would dismiss the children while she burned damp grass in the coal bucket to drive them out. We were always a mess of bums, both with mosquitoes and fleas. At night our beds were full of fleas it seemed. We kept the old fashioned sticky flypaper on the floor by our beds to fasten down a few of them. One round of that and we felt that we really earned that $50 per month.

A flaxburner was something new to me. Dakota raised lots of flax and it is full of oil. These stoves had two drums attached to them which could be removed easily and one had two drums and while one was burning the other was being packed with flax straw, and really packed, until it was one solid mass. The empty drum would then be taken off and the full drum fastened to the stove, which was really a platform with a stovepipe. One drum would usually burn all night and gave out a lot of heat.

My school was entirely Russian children. The best land was taken and proved up on by Russian emigrants. Their women pulled all the wild mustard by hand from the wheat fields. Their houses were built of gumbo soil cut into blocks after it was dried. With this gumbo though, was mixed manure. While the manure and mud were in the soft state, horses were driven back and forth over it to pack and mix and then after it was dry it was cut into blocks and the floorless house was built. The stock was also sheltered in the same kind of building usually right up against their home. They attended the dances and one old bearded Russian was very insistent that he kiss his children's American teacher—ME! I felt that I was in the embrace of a Grizzly and was about to be devoured.

My worst experience, I believe, was the time I was lost on these endless prairies. I wanted to make the trip to our town forty miles away to see about getting to teach there as one of the teachers had taken off for civilization, completely fed up it seemed. The town had around 400 souls. The Bar D owner hitched up his best team, old rack of a buggy, lantern at my feet as well as a footstone. He buried me in his big sheepskin lined coat and set me off assuring me the team would guide me anywhere I wanted to go, but advising me to start back before daylight on my homeward drive. The weather was beautiful. It was early November. I had no trouble in reaching the little village, doing my errand, some visiting and had a good night's sleep. I was well on my way by daylight. The weather was clear and bright and not cold. My lantern was burned out and I did not replenish it before I started but did heat my stone or my friends did for me.

At noon the skies became hazy, then clouded and a light snow started but became huge flakes within the hour or so. The horses kept up a steady gait and I was not concerned at all until later I noticed that the team seemed confused, sort of, weaving back and forth as though they were off of the trail. There were no fences and, of course, the trail had been obliterated for some time. I gave them their heads but still they seemed uncertain. The only marker I could remember was occasionally a pile of rock that some homesteader had picked from his land and piled up. After awhile, when dusk began to crowd in, I was worried. I began to think of all the bad things I had done and of the stories I had heard of being lost on these same plains. Several times we would bump up against an object but on investigation it would be one of those pile of rocks. I knew straight up and that was all and I came to the conclusion that was about all the horses knew, too. I just prayed that it would not get bitter cold and that the wind would not rise, for then there would be a real blizzard with all the snow.

Everything now was as quiet as closing your eyes. Then, suddenly we bumped into something again and I could see the outline of a cabin or so it seemed. Getting out of the rig, I discovered that it was an empty homesteader's shack. Of course, it would be unlocked as everyone left their shacks that way and the door opened easily and in the dim light I saw an oil lamp on a table, but how about a match? I hadn't any but diving into the pockets of Dave's coat I came up with a handful. Thank God, he was a smoker! I lit one, praying the lamp had oil in it as I lifted the chimney. It had, but the chimney was so smoked, only a dim light could filter through, enough that I could see that there was an old stove and a few chunks of coal on the floor. There was a pile of old papers, an old bedstead with a tick filled with what I knew would be spelt straw and a part full bucket of frozen water. There was an old broken chair which I finished breaking up with a rusty old ax. With the papers and the chair splinters, I soon had a fire. I very gingerly put on a small piece of coal. I must make that last for I might find myself there for some days. The team was standing quietly, tired out with their plugging through snow. I was glad that I knew how to unhitch them. I was going to bring them in with me but did you ever try getting a bronc through a door when it was strange? I knew if I could get one in, the other would follow. But I tugged and tugged on the bridle and then, at last, getting behind him and punching with an old broom, he made one lunge and just missed tearing the door down and then the other meekly followed. They made for the bed tick and began munching on the spelt straw, showing through the slit in the tick. Evidently, it had been newly filled.

When they were quiet, I brought in the remains of my lunch and the plunder from the buggy and then looked around to see if I could locate myself. There was a box of crackers tied on a wire near the ceiling. Mounting the table, I was able to get it. It had stale crackers in it all right but hard as bullets. I looked at the papers and saw they had been sent to a Milo Woods and I nearly jumped for joy for I knew him and knew this must be his claim. Its not more than 2 miles from the Bar D, but when I tried to think what direction the ranch would be and tried to remember what end of the shack Milo's door was (as we had been there on different occasions) I just couldn't. If I should start out for the ranch, I might go right in the opposite direction so the best bet for me was to stay put till morning and maybe my directions would come to me. The horses would help keep the room warm, too. Then, they might start out from the ranch to hunt me, as they knew I should be back there even now and would be more anxious especially as it had snowed. I had strict orders when to start back and then, too, I had to be there Monday morning for my school. So I was hopeful they would start out looking for me.

The light was too dim to read the papers and magazines around me. I prayed my kerosene would last until daybreak. The horses were noisy, munching the straw and rattling the harness. I dozed now and then in the one old chair left, awaking in time to add another little chunk of coal. I thought it had stopped snowing, looking through the dirty window and the horses were trying to sleep, too, with their lower lips hanging from them like scoops. After awhile, the oil did burn out and the dark was alive, prowling like a cat. After hours it seemed, daylight crept in, creeping up stealthily and the horses again munched Milo's bed. The room was full of their stench. I munched again on some of the crackers, wondering just what to do. Then I heard voices and wheels creaking in the snow. Never was a sound more heavenly! The ranch boys had come. They had waited until morning and if I was not holed up somewhere on the trail, they were going on to town to trace me. It was an experience I did not forget in a hurry. The funny part was that I was so near the ranch and perhaps the horses would have gotten me there all right had we not stopped at the shack. Dave said they would have.

And that was Dakota in 1905. It is only about 90 percent prairie and it is not wholly treeless. The watercourses have a fringing of shrubs and once in awhile a real tree. The prairie is natural grassland that millions of buffalo once roamed. The prairie now has been settled, named, tamed, plowed, and broken to harness. That is hard to believe on the lonely stretches where the homes still are several miles apart and unbroken distances pull vision beyond the grasp of the mind. But signs of the plow are always in evidence and reminders of the taming; the fence lines now are constant companions. The sense of land creeps in and grows until it dominates all else and that land apparently limitless, serene, indifferent, enduring the surface scratchings of man under the great rounded bowl of the sky. The day wanes and the sun drops to the horizon and an unbelievable glory of color claims the sky. The old longhorns and the cowboy are gone but Dakota is still spreading out its wonderful acres to the very horizon, it seems. The last time I went through this big lonely state was on a westbound train chasing the sunset. It was a long time ago, too, and it seemed I closed the door behind me on this majesty of space and I bowed my head and felt its grandeur and whispered, "Goodbye Dakota and thank you," and the train sped on feeling its way with its long headlight beam piercing the darkness.

Then my thoughts turned again back to Iowa and my childhood days. Funny how events come like that. This time I was seeing Roy and I picking potato bugs, those big and black-yellow things that destroyed the plant. We would trudge wearily up and down the rows, dropping the bugs into oil that was in the cans we carried.

Then seeing Mother frowning at harness cleaning time, she never complained, but once a year, Father would drag the harness into her clean kitchen and pour on and rub in the thick grease. Most of it went into the leather but there was plenty left for the floor, too. The harness was as slick as a shell game operation. Mother would roll up her sleeves and down on her knees trying to scrub up the grease with her always present soft yellow soap, muttering to herself, "Thank Heaven, not till next year again!"

Then again, while the train rolled on, I was back in my childhood. This time carpet rags. There were always carpet rags to sew. Everything that was worked to shreds was used for carpet rags. I learned to sew them at a very early age. They were strips of cloth sewed together and then rolled into big balls and Mother seemed to always have big gunny sacks filled with these balls. All stored upstairs or in the attic, filled with sediment or sentiment, the attic I mean. Then it was a trip to the weaver. Sometimes Mother braided these rags and made them into rugs. Later she learned to outline pretty patterns on gunnysacks and with a wooden hook pull the colored yarn (dyed as she wanted them) through and then she would shear the loops after the rug or sack was punched full of rags. We thought the finished product was out of this world.

Little boys always wore knee pants and were they proud when they had their first long pants and suspenders. I loved nice clothes and always resented the long sleeved aprons I had to wear to school.

Then there were our circus days. After Roy and I saw our first circus, we rigged up a rope in the haymow for "tight rope" walking and a trapeze and Roy insisted that I walk the tight rope with my open little parasol. Good thing there was plenty of hay under me, for one step or two and I landed. I was equally inept on the trapeze where I was supposed to "skin the cat." We charged three pins for the neighboring kids (pins were 5 cents a paper then of about 100 pins.) I was also the "fat lady" of the show. I donned Mother's Mother Hubbard dress and stuffed it with pillows round and about me with hands and feet and head visible. I dared not move. Our show business came to a quick end when Ray was put behind an old sheet with a hole cut in it and Ray's head shoved through and the youngsters, for a pin, could throw eggs at him. He was crying to the top of his lungs and was pretty badly smeared when Mother rushed in. The result is history.

The one chore we dreaded, on Sunday morning before dressing for Sunday school, was running down a rooster for Sunday dinner. Why we did not catch them off of the roost at night, I'll never know. Sunday morning,

Father would call to us and pick out the rooster we were to race to death and then turn us loose. Panting and out of breath, we kept up the chase trying to get him in a fence corner. The poor rooster would at last stumble from sheer exhaustion, and then we two little friends would close in on him and grab. We would usually run a nail into a foot, cut a toe with glass, or get a stone bruise, but we kept right on going, knowing that Father's chew of tobacco would relieve the hurt.

Bumblebee stings were another pleasure we indulged in. I would dare Roy, or more often he would dare me, to stand over a wasp's nest until he counted ten and he would give me a part of his chicken for Sunday dinner. I would try, but he would count so slowly, like the preacher giving the blessing when he came to Sunday dinner with us so hungry and anxious to eat.

Oklahoma

After my homesteading experience, my folks decided they would like to go to Oklahoma and start anew in that, then, new country. The famous "run" had been made for homestead lands but there was plenty left. So a sale was called and they sold about all they had, taking Ray and Guy with them. Roy had a good job at the blacksmith shop and was going to buy his own shop so he stayed in Guthrie Center and I was now in a lawyer's office learning the abstract game. The folks, on arriving in Oklahoma, bought some lots in the then new town of Cashion. They were real homesick and it was not long before Mother took down with typhoid fever and I went to her at once. The town was a desolate place with a few shacks on the lots, grassless and treeless and a few hastily constructed stores, hotel, and a big JAIL. Father and the two teenage boys had bought two teams and were freighting to and from Guthrie, the capital. They would be gone from three days to a week. I remember the soil was a bright red and the heat was terrific.

There was no train at that time and the day it first came in, the whole town was out to meet it; the women in calico clad, and the men in overalls. There was no law nor order, one lone cowboy, being the marshal, and he was usually a wreck after a Saturday night with torn clothes, black eyes, bloody face, from trying to arrest the lawbreakers and getting them in jail and he sure jailed them, too. He was a single man and seemed to like me from the first. He was known as Texas Bill and that is the only name I can remember. He did help me a lot with Mother sick in bed, since Father and the boys were away so much. One day, he told me that some convicts were loose and to keep the shack door locked. He was so concerned that he sat all night one night outside in an old spring seat. We appreciated it, as we were afraid in that then lawless town.

We also experienced one of Oklahoma's cyclones. It came early in the night and shacks were being hurled at one another all over the town. Ours was standing it pretty well. Suddenly we heard a loud pounding on our door and a call for help. Ray cautiously opened it against the wind and a man plunged in stark naked. Ray hastily threw a robe around him. He had been hurled out of his bed when his shack took flight. He never did find his clothing.

Mother improved slowly. By that time, she had enough of Oklahoma so we decided to go back to Iowa and not being able to sell the wagons nor the mules, we outfitted them the best we could with canvas tops and a few necessary things for camping, we started by covered wagon—HOME. We had mules. Father had traded the horses for them as the natives told him that mules would stand the trip much better.

Texas Bill, my cowboy, felt as deserted as a single shoe. We slipped away as easy as money one bright fall day before daylight. What was our surprise when out a few miles, a man galloped up alongside and it was Bill. He rode along with us that day to Guthrie. We crossed the river as the sun came up and it tied the water in long gold ribbons and the dawn was suddenly husked of its beauty. The little lake was passed further on, and it was lovely, too. The water seemed to be giggling in the sunlight, pleased at our going, perhaps. Yes, Oklahoma was beautiful too, in a wild sort of a way. As we neared Guthrie, orphaned leaves were swirling up the streets. I have never forgotten Texas Bill, his natural chivalry, tenderness underneath a rough exterior and unafraid of danger when right and order was to be enforced. When he bade us goodbye, with promises to write, and held out his hand to grasp mine, I saw tears and I still see the sun laying on his eyelids like pennies of warm gold. He turned swiftly and was soon lost in the distance. Many years later, the folk's lots had oil on them and two paying wells, I believe.

Mother was tired, so we stayed in Guthrie overnight. In those days, the town had what is known then as bunkhouses for the public. The bunks were one above the other like Pullman sleepers with husk mattresses or straw. Also, a kitchen with all utensils for cooking and stoves and families would stay overnight and were welcome to use all these facilities for free. The next day, we continued our journey eastward and northward. We stopped at houses along the way and bought our provisions. Mother improved right from the first. I think we made an average of about twenty miles a day as we were in pretty hilly country. When we came to the Arkansas River, we did a big washing right out in the river, pounding the overalls on the rocks for a washboard.

The journey was uneventful and it took several weeks. We went to bed with the braying of the mules and woke up to the same music. The scenery was lovely and changing. The water in the rivers was rollicking and blue, especially the Arkansas River. The evening sun seemed to be making love to all of Nature. Trees were restless with small breezes. Old rail fences sprawling drunkenly by the roadside until fields in the dusk would seem to lose the reeling fences—houses drawing their window shades down like eyelids and the tired eyes of day were closed and we would camp for the night.

In Kansas, the mules would have to have new shoes every few days. The flint-covered hills were pretty rough on them. Did you know a mule is a lovable thing? They are as clever as can be, too. You can't follow them over four states and not love them. They give you plenty of time to see the scenery, too. Ray and Guy really lived on watermelons on that trip and, oh boy, what watermelons! Every campsite was full of rinds with their broad empty grins. We picked out nice camping places, usually by a river if one was anywhere near. We liked to listen to the river's constant plaint through the night under big trees, too, with their branches overhead locked like lover's fingers, soundless breathing, whispers of the soft winds—trees, dark ghosts in the silence of night talking to me in unheard voices. The silence was often broken by an owl lost and star saddened as it cried out against the night. Like the sound of nightlife, the soul-tearing cry of the turtle dove, lovely friendly chirp of crickets, and the flash of fireflies. All these things helped to heal the scars upon the soul and most of us do have some of these scars.

Some days when we had an unusually nice campsite, we would stay over a day to rest Mother and the mules or if the morning woke with a sulk, turning into a pout and finally breaking into tears. We did not start out in a rain. The rain in camp rested us, too. We picked wildflowers along the way to brighten the wagons, sometimes even the dandelions, a few left to button the sod to the still warm earth. Along in Missouri, in her hills, Nature had painted her masterpiece and framed it with old picturesque rail fences and called it, "Missouri."

Mother was getting trail weary and sometimes she would bristle like a porcupine when we tried to dictate to her. We wanted her to conserve her strength for our homecoming. We had written Roy to rent us a house and get some furniture that we had to have and Mother and I could fill in later, so we were sure of a place to live on our arrival. I would have my old job back and the boys would be put in school. We ate like wolves and the trip had been fine for us all.

Home Again

We celebrated when we got into Iowa. We camped in a farmer's yard that night by his invitation. His wife brought us out a berry pie, fried chicken, some homemade bread right out of the oven, and a gallon of rich milk. We had a feast! The children of the home were out, too, wringing the last ounce of play from the day. Then they came to the wagons playing games with us and asking hundreds of questions, it seemed. How good and wonderful these people were, housed there in their own little world. They had a beautiful lake on their farm filled with fish and wanted us to stay over and fish, but we were on the last lap of our journey and were very anxious to get home. The lake looked like a memo pad, as the wind scribbled idle messages on it and one message for me was to always send these gentle people a gift and a message for Christmas. I did until their family scattered and the home was no more. Never will I forget that welcome given to weary road worn travelers along the way. Why aren't more folks like that? Please God help me to remember, too.

The next day as we stopped at a tiny village to make some coffee, we noticed a mob of children gathered around some central object, and lo and behold, it was the Bear Man. I had nearly forgotten the old traveling Bear Man. We had him, too, as children. Back in those days, the Bear Man was a great event; he would seemingly appear from nowhere leading his bear. Then when night came or rather the eventide, the bear was led out on some corner street and would dance like crazy to mouth organ music or sometimes even to the jews harp, a small instrument held between the teeth while one finger thumped the wire protruding from one end. The tune, of course, had to be whistled by the operator. Now back to the bear. After his dance, the bear padded along after his master to their camping place followed by all the children, same as the Pied Piper. The old man always passed his tin cup after each dance and the youngsters gladly dumped in their pennies to see it all over again. I wonder now how he even fed the bear on the small pittance he gleaned from the crowd. Their lodging was cheap, as they would go to some weed covered deserted lot and camp for the night.

Roy and I constantly teased our parents to buy us a bear. I was always planning what I wanted to do when

I grew up. I wanted to be a parachute jumper from a balloon, a pal of a bear, a snake charmer, rope walker, and a bareback circus rider so I could wear a spangled suit and tights and travel the country. All these aspirations caused my Mother a bit of concern. We camped that night, after the bear dancing, in a grove on the nice farm.

The weather changed in the night, as it so often happened in Iowa, weather changes without warning. Iowa's weather, though, was quite different than when we were children. Father always was scanning the skies in winter watching for "sun dogs," (whatever they are) so he could tell what the coming weather would be. He was the weatherman of our neighborhood. We could always count on the "January thaw" of a few days. We would then lose our three and four foot icicles that had hung on the roof edge. Our windows were never free from frost and how we loved to copy the figures that Jack Frost had painted on our windows—flowers, Indians, houses, and all took on life to us after we had copied them on our cardboards from the windows. There were always new pictures to interpret. Jack Frost was almost as real a person to us as was Santa Claus. What winters! Father always backed the house with straw and dirt nearly up to the windows to keep out the winter cold. There were days, even when it was terribly cold, that we would load up in the bobsled and go to some neighbors for an all day "quilting bee."

Then there was the box social at the schoolhouse where the men would bid on the boxes prepared by women and girls and the highest bidder won the box and had to eat and share it with the owner. Often the man knew the owner of the box and if there was a contestant, the bids would run high, maybe then to the big sum of one dollar and perhaps a bit more. If the man was trying to win the gal, then they were out, one to the gent and one to the lady, different colored ribbons on all and the idea was to match the ribbons and the corresponding one was the one to eat supper with.

Other amusements and games were, "Going to Jerusalem," a row of chairs being placed together alternating facing each other with an odd chair, and one less than the number playing. They'd march around the chairs sighing some ditty and when the leader said, "Stop," all scrambled for a chair and, of course, always one would be left and so it continued. The game of, "Authors," was then very popular. Blind's Man's Bluff was another party game, an object being hidden in the room and the blindfolded one guessing and going to the object. When near, cries of, "Warm," or "Warmer," if they approached closer, and so on until the object was located. The idea was that the person was hypnotized. Then, "Button, Button, Who Has the Button," had one person with a button between his clasped hands going to each person and placing his closed hands between the closed hands of each person and he was supposed to drop the button to one of these persons, which he did, and one had to guess who had it. That person had to repeat the performance of the first and so on. And, of course, "Post Office," a real kissing game, which seems to be played even now at some parties. That was our entertainment.

We, too, had a magazine or two to look forward to like, "*The Youth's Companion*," "*Comfort*," "*Household*," for Mother, and, "*The Almanac*." Wonder what children of today would think of such entertainment? How would young couples of today like to take a hammock and go to some grove or woods, hang it between trees and enjoy a few hours visit or read together some book they like, a Bertha Clay novel, perhaps, or go for a Sunday afternoon's walk and if there was a new house being constructed, walk out to see it and see what new things might be incorporated in its construction? Maybe, they'd plan their own, for we never heard of apartments in those days in the little towns. In the evening, the beau would call for his lady and go to Epworth League and then church services afterward.

Remember the palm leaf fans we always carried? Sometimes the whole congregation seemed to be waving like a palm grove. Mother gave me a little folding fan and I did not know how to open it, nearly breaking it while pulling it straight out. Mother saw me just in time. That morning, at Sunday school, I certainly did my share of waving. All little girls wore a nice sash for Sunday and mine was blue brocaded silk to be worn with my white dress. Then it was folded neatly and put in the bureau until the next Sunday. Our Sunday dresses, in the summer, were always white and usually Decoration Day was the first time that we could wear them, starting the summer season. My Sunday shoes were high, scalloped tops and buttoned. My everyday shoes had brass strips across the toes. I was supposed to keep my Sunday shoes always–shiny black. I had; also, my lacy little mitts for Sunday wear. They pulled over the hands and wrists and just covered the upper half, leaving the fingers bare. My hat seemed to always have long ribbon streamers.

We were just beginning to hear of automobiles and were told that a certain morning one was to go through our town early. I remember we set the alarm so that we would not miss seeing it as the road went right by our place that it was to pass. At daylight, yards were filled with people watching for it. At last, it came in at the dizzy speed of 15 miles per hour! Well, we had seen an automobile and not long after, the banker and one or two other well–to–do citizens went to Chicago and brought back an automobile. They were guided by a stick affair instead of a wheel and were high up from the ground. What a time these folks had to learn to drive them and runaways was an everyday affair for awhile. Horses were panicked by them. I remember of seeing a livery team jump a fence and leaving the buggy on end and the driver teetering around and swearing profusely. One man bumped into a brick wall and kept repeatedly bumping into it back and forth as the tires struck the wall. He was beside himself with fright and madly grabbing at every gadget on sight on the car to stop it. He eventually found the right thing to do and stopped it from its mad bucking.

We had never heard of a beauty parlor although there were some hairdressing shops in Des Moines. We washed our hair faithfully once a month with an egg beaten frothy and added to the water. The rinse contained lemon juice or a dollop of vinegar. A few tried dyeing their grey hair with walnut juice, procured from boiling the walnut hulls until the water was black and the Old Magnolia Balm was used for painting the face a ghostly white. Our lips and cheeks were rosy from sheer health and once in awhile gals who were a bit pale, tinted their lips and cheeks with a bit of red calico moistened.

Black hose were worn by everyone. The cotton ones were 10 cents a pair and the lysle, for Sunday, were 25 cents per pair. Anyone who had a pair of black silk hose was really "swell," as we termed it then. They were $1.00 per pair.

Ironing was really some job those days. We usually wore two white petticoats, ruffled and plaited halfway up to the waist and very full. These were starched stiff and ironed really wet. Everything had tucks and lace insertions as was our panties, full as skirts and just as full of tucks, insertions and lace. Our corset covers, the same, too. Our dresses touched the ground and when we danced we clutched a handful of skirt in one hand while we hung onto our partner with the other. Sometimes we had a skirt holder, a little gadget that fastened to the belt and one rod grasping the long skirt. In rainy weather, we used the same firm clutch and were sure only ankles could show and so nervous if a man was walking behind us on the street. Raglins were very popular, a long full coat that really covered us.

Going back to our return from Oklahoma. Back to Iowa, the heart of the heartland. We appreciated it more than ever with its great asset-soil. Great wealth comes from that soil. Gently the land rises and falls always tilting its fertile face to the sky. Iowa people do feel intensely possessive about their land and rightly so, an abundant land. Its life and its people are balanced and solid. It is a country of the small town with an average comfortable life. There are no immense fortunes, neither was there real poverty. It had the highest standard of living for its area in the world and a quarter of all the best land in America. Two big rivers are its friends, although, of the Missouri, the old saying is that, "It's too thick to drink, too thin to plow," but Iowa is just right to plow, no waste, no mountains, no swamps, or no big forests. The rivers are everywhere; more like streams and all along these streams are willow, maples, elm, walnut, butternut trees, and wild grapes clinging to them like a bride. So many little streams like veins in a wonderful body.

Winter, I know is a savage season, or used to be. Blizzards that would rattle your very teeth. Frost goes deep into the ground and the snow really piles up in huge drifts. But spring is always not far behind and the seeds then jump in sheer joy. May morning is here and the sun drips a golden life on the soil and seeds wiggle out with joy. The corn shoots, later, make the land look like a tufted quilt. The baby pigs squeal and frolic while their mothers are munching their grain, while putting bacon on their thick sides. Summer? Oh yes, the old state turns into a sizzling skillet with midnight about only 2 degrees cooler. The beds are dragged out on the lawn to get a breath of air, but the corn jumps up an inch or two every hot night in the awful heat. But her fall, that delightful Indian summertime, like no place else on earth. Fields still and quiet as a smile, everything ripening and begging to be harvested. This golden season, sad, but very beautiful. Muted leaves that fall, whispering sadly, but bearing a freight of autumn rain.

We were back in time for the County Fair. It really doesn't change much and even now it is almost the same only folks dressed differently. I loved it as a child and now at eighty-four years, I look forward to going almost as eagerly as I did years and years ago. Mother used to say, "The same old bull and the same old pumpkin." Usually, we were out to the barn first with its rows of Jerseys, Guernsey's, Swiss and Black Angus with their shiny, glistening bodies, all combed and groomed. Oh, those giant hogs, litters of darling little pigs with their contented grunts, and beautiful plumed chickens all resenting the close pens. What a cacophony of sound! Turkeys with their gobble, gobble and the cackling of hens. The best and finest of Iowa's vegetables were stretched out along the sides of the farmer's display. Squash and pumpkins, almost bursting with pride at their huge size. Tall corn reaching upward, too, in pride. Then in the woman's building, there were women standing around awaiting to see who had the blue ribbons on those delectable cakes, pies, cookies, and great loaves of homemade bread and rolls. Then the rows of pickles, jellies, fruits and vegetables were tantalizing and inviting. There were not many canned vegetables years ago. The farm wife dried her vegetables those days and anyone who has not tasted dried corn with oodles of cream on it has truly missed something. The machinery sheds interested all, too, and there again the machinery on display would be very meager compared to the wonderful, almost human, machinery of today. There would be little stands everywhere selling pink lemonade at, "Only 5 cents per glass," and stands where one could buy a bunch of seaweed or peacock feathers to adorn the wall. Then the phonograph man with his little stand where you could put on the earphones and listen to music and only one at a time could listen for 5 cents. Later, they had them with two earphones.

The men and boys would all hurry to the racetrack where horses were jogging with their light sulkies and the old time horsemen with their legs straddling the shafts and their visor caps protruding out over their faces. I loved the races, too. Roy was lightweight and I remember he used to ride for the running races with his little jacket of blue satin. For a long time, Mother did not know that he rode. She quickly put a stop to that. At first they tied him on.

The farm folks, of course, would be out in full force along with the townsters. I loved to watch the farmers with their earnest tired faces visiting, gossiping and giving their experiences with their mutual problems. They loved to watch the steer judging, the big draft horses trying to out pull a neighbor's team. The young men were there, too, in force, big and awkward in their Sunday clothes, coming in sheepishly from the "girlie" show or a gypsy fortune-telling tent. The children came in shouting joyfully from the merry-go-round. Then the baskets of food pulled out from the farm wagons while the women spread out the red and white checkered tablecloths and piling on the fried chicken, cakes, pies, pickles, deviled eggs and coleslaw. Loaves of bread and "buns" and each one buttered and jammed his own bread, as no one seemed to make sandwiches then. Those Iowa farm women knew how to bake no mistake about that.

After dinner, the young folks hurried away to the dance pavilion, a few rough boards put together and overhead green boughs from the nearby trees were placed on an improvised roof. The fiddle would mournfully "tune up" and with someone to "chord" on the organ, the dance began. Long skirts were swishing and ribbons flying like miniature rainbows and then "Doce–de–do and you know where," and a rush to the benches, swains puffing and girls pink and smiling from their mad dancing. In a few moments, the sweet strains of "Over the Waves," waltz or, "Beautiful Blue Danube," and couples paired off and those in love gazed tenderly into each other's eyes as the sobbing music wafted out on the hot and dusty air. The waltz then was a lovely graceful thing with its slow intoxicating rhythm. Was there and is there anything like a Country Fair? Long may they live.

Back from Oklahoma and its roughness and newness, I felt that I was ready to make Iowa my home forever and a day, but after awhile something was lacking. I was restless and disturbed. The wanderlust was on me again. I had almost bargained for a small store, in fact, had even invoiced it, but now I felt that I must go. Grace, who had homesteaded with me in North Dakota, came to me one day and said, "Have you heard of the Carey Land Act in Idaho? You know, Iva, I want to go. I think it would be a lark, not like the long pull in Dakota. The law requires but five weeks homesteading and only 50 cents per acre to pay down and then you buy water with 25 years to pay like taxes. It is an irrigation project. I will bring you the literature to look over. Then we can go into it more thoroughly."

Maybe, this is what I want, I thought. "All right, Grace, we'll talk it over." I dreamed of it day and night. I had been West but once and that a two weeks vacation out to the Grand Valley in Colorado where many of the Guthrie County folks had gone. I was thrilled with the trip and had packed a few peaches to help defray expenses. I knew I could never buy peach land at $3000 an acre so I had no dreams about locating there. On that trip, I took the Pike Peak's trip on a burro, 24 hours in going 24 miles, but what a lark! We rode those mountain canaries all night and arrived on the top at daybreak for the sunrise and believe me, it was worth the ride. It was in August and we were all nearly frozen. I'll never forget the glory of that sunrise on the top of the world. Heaven couldn't be far away!

After informing ourselves pretty thoroughly about Idaho and its possibilities, Grace and I embarked on another adventure. No girl ever had a better pal than she was. Idaho, anyway called to me, for I had my girlhood sweetheart buried out there and my heart was partly there, too.

When I was but sixteen, I met and loved this boy and helped him financially to go to Idaho as he had TB and needed the mountain country. I had promised to go to him when he sent for me. But it was not to be for he died out there in that big lonely country. Some day I meant to keep my promise and go to him. After fifty years, I found his lonely grave. I had kept my promise. It was a lovely spring day and I walked slowly along a country road to a cemetery in Idaho. Silently and reverently, I entered the gates and with the aid of the caretaker found the grave. As I stood there by the monument my thoughts went back along the chain of years. Once again, I was a young happy girl loving and being loved.

The future looked bright and then the blow came. The doctor said he must go West and up in the mountains. Once again I visualized the train that carried him away from me to death or health; and it was—death. Years sped away but his memory was the one bright spot in my life. Other men, so far, had meant nothing to me. And now I was with him. Kneeling softly by him, I whispered, "Paul, I am here." The invisible hand of the wind seemed to stroke the green velvet of the grave and moaned a sad farewell. Birds above in the trees sang a sweet requiem and the sun filtered through the leaves to caress the white hair of the woman—me. It was thus he spoke to me (for the dead do speak, you know). In the sun, the wind and the bird song, I felt his nearness, his dearness. With a long last look and a hushed, "Goodbye," I turned away again to the dusty road and the world outside the gates. Looking back now, over fifty years, I had kept my word. I had gone to him. Why do I digress like this? Just spots of golden memories loom up every now and then.

CHAPTER IV

Westbound Train

(1907 On-ward)

———— ◆ ————

Well, Grace and I purchased our tickets for Idaho. At the time, we purchased a round trip ticket for $32 clear to Seattle and back. We bought a round trip so that we could come back if we had made a mistake. We were simply thrilled the whole trip and our spirits were high especially when we entered the mountains with all their immensity and grandeur, then miles and miles, endless miles, it seemed of sagebrush. Idaho, the land of the sage.

Had we made a mistake? This seemed like the end of the world. We were nearing our destination and the terrain seemed to get more lonely, more bleak and desolate with every mile. When the conductor called, "Twin Falls," we knew we were at the end of the long trip. We pulled into a little depot and the platform was filled with a very mixed crowd of humanity, women brown as Indians, men of all sizes and makeup, mostly overalled—straw hats, big cowboy hats, caps and some derbies all crowding up to the train, expectant, eager. Most of the men were meeting families who were joining them from the East.

We had no one to meet us so we trudged up the newly made sidewalk until we came to a sign, "Rooms for Rent," and it looked as if it were quite respectable. Of course, it was newly built. We contacted the red-headed landlady, who questioned us as to where we came from, what we expected to do. Then, she informed us that she did not like to take in women roomers who were alone, but that she rather liked our appearance and graciously gave us a room. We felt better and were anxious to see the little western town that so far didn't look like most of the pictures in the literature. We were ravenously hungry, too. We found a restaurant on Main St., a street short with dust an inch deep on the board sidewalk. We went into quite a large Japanese restaurant and had a very good meal.

Everyone was so friendly and helpful. We liked the atmosphere of the place at once, but my, how crude and new everything was! But, we had survived the Dakota plains and we felt this could be no harder and were assured that there were no blizzards, no tornadoes, nor forty-below weather. So we were quite happy when we returned to our room and as our landlady was a very garrulous person, we soon knew a lot about the town and most of its inhabitants. She was a character, as her face always looked rumpled, as if she had slept all night in her thoughts. She was one of those persons who like to be first with the worst so we were duly warned who was and who wasn't and it was mostly wasn't. Lots of folks to talk to, at least. In Dakota, there were many days when I saw no human being and yet had no sense of loneliness for there I had an integral though humble part in the great design of nature, a feeling of kinship to forces far above and beyond me. This comes, I believe, only to those who live out of doors. There miles and miles of nothing but miles and miles. Out here space is filled with Brain, Brawn or Bust. Maybe, we lacked brain and brawn but we sure did not intend to bust. Success must and would be ours.

The next morning we went into a real estate office on the first floor of the building where we had our room. We were anxious to find and locate some of this Carey Act Land. As we opened the door, we were met by a big man, pompous and seemingly very sure of himself. He certainly had built himself a nice bay window by "do–it–yourself," method and the tools, a knife and fork! He motioned us to chairs and then went back to his big chair wiggling like the south end of a happy hound. It was later than we thought for the clock hands like scissors had snipped the day in half. The big man, after a few questions as to where we were from and what we had in mind, smilingly pointed to a fine–looking man who was busy at the wall phone. "Frank here will take care of you in a minute. He is our outside man here and knows the country like a book. It is my lunch time so please excuse me and I'll see you again, I hope," and with that he ponderously rose and teetered out.

I carefully studied the man at the phone and he was my ideal of a truly western man, large, but not fat and his face was like a fine piece of granite, chiseled in perfect lines with full lips and every muscle rippling as he walked towards us with a smile that lit up his whole face and the kindest most expressive eyes one could ever wish to see. I trusted him instantly and a message seemed to emanate from him, a message to me. He was very graceful in his movements–he just seemed to panther along the floor. He greeted us in such a friendly manner and not hurried as if he would give us the whole day if need be. He just made you feel special. We told him briefly what we wanted. He informed us that very little Carey Act Land was to be had now but he still did know of some across the river. It was not as desirable as some on this side of the river (the Snake River) but we wanted to see the land anyhow and get it if possible. So arrangements were made for the next day to go, some twenty-odd miles or more. Again, that peculiar electric shock when he shook my hand as we left the office.

As we came out, everything was aglow–the sun seemed brighter, the skies bluer. "What is the matter with you?" I said to myself. I was drawing my own CONFUSIONS and believe me I was confused, too! This had never happened to me since I met Paul years and years ago. The smoke was even soaring out of the chimneys like ribbons along a wedding aisle. The leaves swirling about seemed to be challenging my feet to run and jump for joy and the sunshine on the dusty sidewalk was a soft powdering of sifted gold. I felt close to him, like ivy to a stone wall.

Gracie's voice brought me back to reality as she said snidely, "Come out of it Iva. I thought you were invulnerable. I'll bet he is a cool Daddy with all the girls or else he already has a cute little wife. If he IS a bachelor, he must be the souvenir of some gal who found someone better at the last minute. But I can see that right now, pal of mine, it is 'Tibi splendet focus'—yes sir, for you the hearth fire glows right now, but girlie mine, we are after land. Remember?"

I said to her in reply, laughingly, I hoped, "I can dream, can't I?" I did snap out of it then but in some secret way, I KNEW he was my man. I someway knew that happiness, like loaves of bread all stacked up, was there for me.

At dinner that night Grace said, "Iva, this is the first time since Paul's death that I have seen you a bit interested." I did not answer for I was surprised at myself. As we went to our plain little room the copper sun was westerning. I could not sleep and the stars trembled like a lavalier from an invisible necklace as I watched through the one little window. Gracie's words that he might be married pricked like a misplaced pun. Well, I would soon know. Somehow I was almost afraid to ask our landlady. When we awoke, the sun was gnawing into the fog. Grace awoke with a smile but she did not rib me anymore and we hurried down to breakfast.

How hungry we were in this high altitude. I could hardly wait until it was time to start land hunting with our Mr. Wilson (we had learned his name). The sky cleared and then clouded over a bit. Spring seemed to be coming with its hands full of snowflakes after the fog lifted. We arrived at the office a bit early and again were met by the fat man, Mr. Wilson's partner—his hair bristled like iron filings around a magnet, his mouth a down turned ellipse and a horseshoe under his nose. His effusive greeting was a, "Hello ladies." Frank went to the livery stable for the rig. "Hope the day clears for you, queer day, fog, snow sun and sleet. Nothing though for this time of year." He grunted around the office on elephant feet flecking a bit of dust here and there, most of it landing on his stomach, like a big shelf. Then we saw the team drive up, how beautiful they were, high steppers with lovely arched necks and pink nostrils. We went out at once and Mr. Wilson was courtesy itself placing the robe over the wheel so that we would not soil our skirts.

My heart was jumping again and I could feel my face flushing up and shone like the play of Northern Lights. He took my hand as he helped me in and it reminded me of the line, "A baby's hand soft as April weather, but strong enough to hold the world together." Grace broke the silence after the morning greeting with little conversation nothings. "Well, Mr. Wilson, time tootles on and here we are for the great adventure. Right?"

"Yes and I do hope we have what you want. Time doesn't matter, so relax and let's make a day of it," he smilingly answered.

All I could think of was, "What a beautiful team." His eyes sparkled and I knew that we had one thing in common—love for beautiful horses. "I see you admire good horse flesh, too. It is a passion with me."

"I certainly do," I replied and we sped along in the early morning as we had a long drive ahead of us. We noticed little cabins that rode the brow of the occasional hills like lighted liners and marshmallow capped fence posts standing in the light snow. People were building fences out in this spaceless space and trying to make homes. The light homes were welcome beacon lights along this sea of land and brush. Then after a spell, the sun was out bright as my heart. The scenery was beautiful in a wild way. At last, we came to the canyon of the Snake, not like any other canyon in the world. After fifty years, it is still new to me! The cliffs, frowning and threatening, crafted by time and weather. The road was winding and at one place we went right under a huge waterfall, brilliant as a shower of silver and the sun came out brightly as we passed under.

He spoke but once going down this dangerous grade— that is, dangerous it seemed to us. "Don't be frightened, it is perfectly safe and the horses are used to it."

I wanted to tell him that I would ride to Hades and back with him and not be frightened but Grace squealed, "Oh, we love it! Nothing ever frightens us."

I think the horses would have gone over the cliff if he had told them to. They responded to every touch on the lines as if they, too, felt his electric touch. We crossed the Snake River on an old ferry. All the lumber to build Twin Falls had come across on that ferry. It was an old historic ferry—there before Twin Falls was even dreamed of. The Snake is a beautiful but a very treacherous river with all its graceful curves reminding one that "a snake has all the lines". I think I was conscious every minute of the dynamic man sitting beside me and enjoyed that low caressing voice, explaining all the wonders of the new country emphasizing all its future possibilities, foretelling its wonderful future and which has all materialized.

We were thrilled by it all and then came the actual work of looking and locating our land in all the limitless sea of sagebrush. We located our lines by tying a handkerchief to the wheel and counting the revolutions of the wheel. I can't remember now just how many revolutions in a rod. We also found markers giving us the Township, Section, and etc. We then stopped at the little land office of rough boards sitting out in the brush and marking the site of Jerome, Idaho. Now a thriving town of several thousand people, modern in every way. The sagebrush has been taken over by lovely, prosperous homes, fields waving with grain, beets, beans, and other fields producing the best potatoes in the world—potatoes known and famous all over the United States.

How gladly we signed our papers and paid our 50 cents per acre. We were joyful landowners again. We had hot coffee over the little Montgomery stove in the land office, stuffed every few minutes with sage wood or sagebrush as they all called it. We later learned to use sagebrush for fuel, too. We found it much better than buffalo chips. The smell of the sage lingers with me yet as I wander down the lane of memories. We decided not to use our tickets to go on to Seattle as we had planned but to remain in Idaho.

It would take us, anyway, the six weeks to prove up on our land which would mean that we must build a small shack on it and have a few furrows plowed. Mr. Wilson said he would send us a couple of men who would do the work for us. He did and in a few days our shacks were ready. Some folks were staying but a night or two on their land and then prove up. We found some cheap housekeeping rooms and moved to them during our proving up time, going over across the river in a Mormon shack when it was necessary to stay overnight or do some required work. We surely enjoyed our experiences in this wonderful country.

I was seeing Frank Wilson often and going on long drives with him. I was hopelessly in love! Of course, I had found out at once that Frank was a bachelor and successful but had never taken much interest in women. One of our first trips was out to see his new ranch. He had taken up 160 acres of the best land and was constructing a stone bungalow on it. The walls were about half laid. It was constructed from the natural lava rocks and would be very substantial and, yes, very beautiful when completed. Cupid was certainly shooting his arrows recklessly for within three weeks, we were engaged. In the meantime, he wanted us to take charge of the boarding house on his famous Blue Lakes Ranch, right close to Twin Falls. We agreed.

Twin Falls and I.B. Perrine

I am going to digress a bit and tell you something about the man behind Twin Falls, I.B. Perrine. In southern Idaho, Sunny Southern Idaho, as we who love to call it, lies an inland empire, comprising 273,000 acres. This was known once as the Great American Desert, a vast sea of purple sage, somber and forbidding, daring mankind to enter and conquer. One there was who dared, a great pioneer of irrigation, I.B. Perrine, the Father of this Country, as he is known. Through this vast arid waste, flowed a mighty river, winding its crooked way smoothly and softly, then plunging and foaming through mighty canyons which had taken ages for it to hew its way; over great precipices, where its mad turbulent waters formed a mighty cataract 1500 ft. wide with a fall of 210 feet, known as Shoshone Falls. The falls are grand and weird, foaming and thundering over the rocks, caressed by a rainbow by day and by moonlight an aurora gracefully curved over its shining beauty as a benediction. Then on again on its mad restless way to the sea as if in a hurry to leave the great lonely waste of sage behind. Then came our Dreamer, the man with a vision. He could truly say, "Veni, vidi, vici". He did not see the lonely waste. He saw a valley richer than the Valley of the Nile, and El Dorado. He saw as a mirage, fields of waving grain, sleek cattle, and Eden blossoming in all its beauty for mankind—railroads, prosperous farms, and a happy prosperous people. He knew this could be made possible if only he could harness those rushing, life–giving waters. He saw the great falls, also harnessed by the ingenuity of man, generating heat, power and light. His dreams came true, his Eden materialized. From out of all this wild grandeur and loneliness arose the "Garden of Dreams," for today, Twin Falls is the richest, most productive tract in the world, with every convenience one could desire.

Now a bit about this man who accomplished this magic. He was a modest unassuming man, kind and good to all. He came from Indiana when very young—endured the vicissitudes of pioneer life and surmounted obstacles that would have most men quit. "Nil desperandum," was his rule of life. He had been a miner, cowboy and liveryman in the days when livery stables were in vogue. His home was the famous, Blue Lakes Ranch. He first saw the lakes from which his ranch derived its name from the top of the cliff walls far below him shimmering in the sun, water blue as the turquoise sky above them. There was no trail down the steep perpendicular cliff and in order to reach the lakes, he and his pardner rigged up a tackle and lowered themselves, the grub and other plunder down into the canyon. Perrine wrote out his location notices and stuck them up on the rocks. He then headed for Boise (a week's journey on foot) for the purpose of recording his land entry and buying seed as he intended to make his home in the canyon. He had no money and after reaching the stage road, he asked the stagedriver to give him a lift and told the driver of his ambitions and his desire to raise fine fruit. "Well, get in," said the driver, "any kid with a notion like that is sure dangerous to society—hop in and I'll give you a lift to the asylum up there in Blackfoot."

"Thanks," said Perrine, "this is the only time I'll ask you for a lift. I'll buy this stagecoach someday and ride in it whenever I want to." Years later, he did just that. He did raise fruit and such fruit! It took Gold Medal at the Paris Exposition and again at Buffalo, St. Louis and Omaha. The only way he had of getting it out of the canyon in the early days was a steep trail along the canyon wall. Up this trail, he led a single horse packed with fruit in baskets. He found his markets in little towns thirty miles across the sagebrush.

A few years before the city of Twin Falls started, he built a picturesque road down into the canyon to his ranch and one of the wonders of the ranch were the fruit trees here and there among mighty boulders, each tree reached by the little ditches carrying the life–giving water like little fairy visitors, coaxing out bud and blossom and fruit. All the time he was developing this unique ranch, he was dreaming of the possibilities of the then untouched desert all around him. If only that rush of waters could be dammed, hundreds of thousands of acres might be watered. He had the will and determination but where was the money coming from? He made inquires and found out that it would take millions. He must find someone who was willing to trade dollars for desert. His friends thought him crazy but he never gave up. Then he heard that an Eastern millionaire, who was then at Salt Lake, Utah looking for something like his idea.

He lost no time in contacting him and the easterner came and he and Perrine traversed the desert and he, too, caught the "vision." The result of the marriage of "millions" and wild desert produced one of the most productive countries in history. Time alone will tell what this man has wrought. He has gone now and much of the beauty of his beloved ranch has also been sacrificed to modern demands. In blossom time, Blue Lakes Ranch seemed like a fragrant lovely dream faraway from the hurry and struggles of life where rest, beauty and peace reigned. The deep green of the trees, the sparkling, bubbling, glistening waters, changing as the sunlight played upon their changing form, the towering canyon walls and the ethereal blue of the sky, gave one the thought of expansion, uplift and blessedness. To me, it will always seem that way.

I.B. Perrine has given more to more people than many whose names are immortalized in history. Few men have equaled him in actual accomplishment. He built where others razed and destroyed. His name and his work is a monument eternal—I.B. Perrine, our empire builder. I return back to the story.

Now, this was the ranch that Grace and I took charge of the boarding house. It was a grand experience for us and we spent three delightful months there. Grace was a good cook so she took over that job while I took care of the tables. We had about 30 boys to look after. Whenever a stranger came to I.B. Perrine and was out of work, I.B. would send him to the ranch and a job was created for him. Some of the boys were from the city and were in Idaho to homestead or grow up with the West. Few of them were worth their salt as help on the ranch. One boy, I remember from Chicago, was sent out to hoe the garden and he did not know a weed from vegetables and the result was that he hoed up more vegetables than weeds.

Frank was a frequent visitor and with a field–glass we would watch him coming down the grade with his prancing team. The first dance we attended in Twin Falls was on the street, a piece of canvas stretched tightly on top of the dust. The dances were Virginia Reel, French Four and The Cotillion. Music, sweat, dust and laughter were all rolled into one hilarious time.

Major Reed, a very colorful character in those days and a real gallant, rushed to assist a lady who had succumbed to the wild revelry. She was quite fleshy and the major at once tried to unfasten her corset (we wore them tight in those days). She needed air and while he was fumbling with the hooks she started to "come to" but when he tried the bottom clasp, too much bulged out again, and with a disgusted, "Damned if I can see where she packed it away!" He beat a hasty retreat, as he met the icy stares of the woman he so gallantly tried to help and restore. This was the first, "Battle of the Bulge." He never quite lived it down.

Twin Falls had a series of "Firsts" over the years. The first Sunday school was in a tent shaded by willows. The first bakery delivered its goods by a wheelbarrow. The first waterworks consisted of a pump in the little creek and a small wooden tank. The tank would be filled with water during the day and hosed out in the evening to freshen things up a bit before the arrival of the stage. The first Christmas tree was a big sagebrush and all had a hand in decorating it. The first ice was hauled in from a town forty miles away. The first Post Office was a corner in a little store. The mail was dumped in an empty corner and everyone had to kneel down on the floor and sort out his own mail. The first hospital was in a restaurant vacated when the hospital was urgently needed when typhoid fever developed in the new settlement. Two women assumed the responsibility. They secured a spring wagon drawn by broncos and with this makeshift ambulance removed the sick to the makeshift hospital that was furnished by contributions from homes and stores.

The first restaurant was called, the Bucket of Blood. This establishment had four ways of parting the individual from his money—first by sale of liquid refreshments, second, by permitting him to sit in on a game of poker, third by feeding him and fourth if any money was left, by "rolling" him in the corral at the alley extension. Adjoining the dining room was a narrow runway that served as a pigpen—the guests could conveniently throw out the bones and unwanted food through the windows to the pigs. The pigs learned to know by the rattle of knives and forks that "eats" were on and would respond with, "Uhgh, uhgh, uhgh." A short time later the building was raided. The gambling tables were carried out and piled in the street and several loads of sagebrush piled on top and then someone dropped a match on top.

Runaways were a daily affair. One runaway was rather spectacular—the horse when freed from the buggy ran into the back door of a barbershop, and out through the front window. A client was in the barber chair, which by the way, was a doctor's operating chair loaned by the town doctor to the barber. It was said that the barber's nerve was so steady that he never missed a stroke of his razor and his client never moved a muscle but the horse was certainly frightened. There were many notable and colorful characters and well-known people connected with the early history of the little city of Twin Falls. Addison Smith, Senator Borah and William Jennings Bryan were frequent visitors. It was here that Ruth Bryan trying to catch a train as they were leaving and being able to just make it exclaimed, "Well, this is ONE time a Bryan got what they ran for." General Funston was also a guest at the Perrine home and it was my pleasure to have a dance with the General. Mr. Buhl, a Pittsburgh, Pennsylvania Millionaire also dined with us girls, and many writers of note also came looking for material and settings for their stories.

A party was given one night for the workers and the Milner Dam, the dam that was to store the great mass of water to be used for our irrigation. All the workmen from Milner and those who were employed on the construction of the main canals came. Since there were no hotel or public halls and no all night eating places, the workmen contented themselves with liquid refreshments, which were bountifully furnished.

As the night wore on, many of the men were found in the streets and alleys in an almost frozen condition. A number of residents banded together as a police force to look after those who were unable to travel. One saloon had a large barroom possibly thirty feet square and the volunteer police took these individuals into the barroom. The first was laid against the farther wall and the next ones brought in were laid side by side until all the floor space was occupied and there was no opportunity for those still on their feet to line up at the bar for more drinks. It was noon of the next day before the floor was entirely cleared of its occupants.

The first jail in Twin Falls was not much when compared to modern bastilles, but students of criminology might rate it highly in preventing crime. A tunnel had been driven into the wall of the canyon and a door installed. This was the jail and the inmates were always warned that they might be sharing their quarters with rattlesnakes which crawled in from the surrounding area. The door incidentally was never closed very securely. One inmate, incarcerated in this fashion, scarcely waited until his escorting officer had reached the rim–rock on his return, before breaking through the flimsy door. It was never learned in which direction he and other "escaping" prisoners took when breaking jail, but none of them ever returned. The rattlesnakes as jail mates did not appeal to them. When the description of this jail was given out, others who might have become involved with the law gave the place a wide berth.

A few of the citizens set out to investigate the hot water conditions evidenced by surface appearances along the foothills. They got some distance from Twin Falls and as night was approaching, they decided to camp for the night. About midway of the next day, they were ready to start back to town so they unhobbled their horses, preparatory to hitching up and climbing into the canvas covered hack to at least rest their tired feet. They found that one of the horses had eaten lobelia and seemed about ready for horse heaven. What to do?

"We decided to place one set of harness in the hack. The doubletree was haltered to the axle and the uninebriated horse was installed for double duty. We took turns, one leading the horse and another carrying the end of the neck-yoke made vacant by the disabled horse then tethered behind the back. We made speed slowly and were certainly exhausted for we had played horse for over twenty miles." These quotes are the words from one of the men who were on this trip.

Our valley is called the Magic Valley and a very appropriate name it is. It is a sparkling gem in a setting that is magic too. The good earth of Magic Valley belongs to the ages, but the task of reclaiming it—the planning and building of prosperous farms and communities in fifty years- is man's accomplishment.

The area here was covered anciently by lava flows that are now bedrock under the silt that has blown in from surrounding mountains and old lake beds. Before the lava flow the area was a great lake bed or really an inland sea and after that a tropical jungle. Thus the region is a repository of dinosaurs, ammonites, coral and seashells.

Surrounded by the most productive farming land in the world, barring none, fringed by eternal snow-capped mountains and scenic wonders that rival anything on earth, the Magic Valley is a veritable tourist's wonderland. Near Twin Falls is located the famous " Craters of the Moon,"

39 square miles of weird beauty with its mountains of ashes, silent river of lava, smooth and glistening; great waves cooled and hardened in the very act of flowing over some log or boulder. It is impressive and alluring in its lonely and compelling beauty. Robert W. Limbert, well-known explorer, says it rivals the famous lava beds of Vesuvius in Italy and Mauna Loa in Hawaii. Growing out of the desolation of lava, are tiny patches of white flowers, reminding us that even in the desolation of the lives of some of us, there still can arise some little beacon of hope and cheer amid the ashes of wasted lives and blasted hopes. Off from the main road are many trails leading off to some particular point of interest, wonderful, fantastic and weird, defying pen or brush to convey any adequate idea by way of description. Crater mouths at one time roaring in awful and terrific grandeur—a tremendous fire-pit, belching out hot lava, which, rolling down the mountain sides in great thick waves, engulfed everything in its path, leaving rocks, cinders of every conceivable shape with colors strikingly beautiful. Then there are the caves where one can drink clear, icy water. Some are coated with an armor of ice and from their roofs hang pendants of icicles eight-foot long. Another cavern has stalactites covered with fine green moss.

A new crater was found last year—the walls were pitched at such an angle that the whole bowl appeared as a grand stadium which, if filled with seats, would exceed the most flowery dreams of the biggest university anywhere. The inside ring of seats would extend for a mile while the outer circle 400 feet up and some distance back would extend for an even greater distance. It was humanized by the ruins of a tumbling little squatter's cabin. Explorers wore automobile tires on their feet, for lava rocks have a cutting edge like glass and these explorers gave this advice, "When visiting the 'Craters of the Moon,' take a spare tire—for your feet."

Then within three miles from our town is the well-known falls, Shoshone Falls, one of nature's wonders. It has a fall of two hundred twelve feet. In the early days, it was known only to the Indians and seen only occasionally by white men. It held romance insisted we visit the almost then unknown City of Rocks forty miles away. We had to plan on camping out as we went by team and the journey was rough. Part of it was made over the old Oregon Trail, the ruts of the frontier wagons still showing in the brush and desert cactus along the way. Ruts in some places were hub deep. The old trail is all obliterated now.

What a surprise when we entered this now famous, City of Rocks, many of the rocks the size of huge buildings. The beauty and grandeur of this historic site is hard to describe. One must get the feel of it. It embraces four square miles of real fantastic granite formation. It is a city of moods, this silent frowning place. At mid-day, it is glaring, bold and defiant. In the early morning, while it impresses you with its unbroken silence, its age and solidity, yet it is friendly and inviting, as the sun rises above its rocky castles and the strange formations begin to take on life. In imagination you see huge birds, reptiles and animals, and men, too. Then you are eager to climb their rough sides and explore their grizzly old tops for you feel that this is a city that tells no tales and you want to discover for yourself its secrets.

To me, at twilight, especially in the afterglow, is this weird spot at its best. Dark settles down as if to shut out every intruder so that the ghosts of the past may hold their nightly revels. In fancy, you can see the shadowy forms of the immigrant trains, hear the creak of the wagons and see the slowly plodding oxen; lurking Indian faces peer at you from around the rocks. You feel the breath of the crouching mountain lion, then in fear, you too crouch down for you seem to hear ghostly Mephistophelean laughter as the wind rises and moans in this mad scene. It is then deathlike stillness and you hear the wind, shrieking and moaning and laughing insanely, tuning the trees to a whispering orchestra. The silver drippings of moonlight are caressing the old granite monarchs and then and only then, you feel the weird charm of age-old rocks shadowed by billowing cumulus clouds—majestic mountains of the sky.

Our people of Idaho and many other states who have visited Idaho's outstanding attraction are anxious that it be made a national monument and it should be, for not only is it a scenic marvel, but it is rich in historical appeal. Here is where the Old Oregon Trail and the California Trail cross. Here was fought the battle of Almo Creek with the Indians and it, too, is the old camping ground of the 49ers. The names of many of them are still clearly visible on the sides of these rocks and the dates when they camped there, written in axle grease. Many stage robberies were staged here and much of the lost loot is still reported to be hidden here. Here also is the largest pine nut grove in the United States. The Indians still go there for these nuts as they did years and years ago, before the white man. The whole area is fairly reeking with historical lore. The lure and charm of this mysterious whispering country depends on the time of day and the mood of the visitor to get the thrill that must in some way come to every visitor unless he is deaf and blind.

Frank's voice aroused me from my revelry. "A long trip back and the sun is high—ready to leave your enchanted land?"

"Well," I answered, "I guess I would never be ready, for this place sure fascinates me, but we can come back."

"Sure, let's all come back and dig up the treasure," called Grace, "Time tootles on—let's get this packing done and back to civilization." How happy and carefree was our dear Grace and so very, very practical, just the kind of a friend I needed with all my daydreaming. I came back to reality when Frank looked at me with those kindly understanding eyes. Would he always be as patient when I was wool gathering, neglecting to do the dishes or feed the cat? Anyway we would eat, for Frank was an expert with bacon, eggs, and the coffeepot.

It has its "Lover's Leap" too. It is however, true, that an Indian brave many years ago did leap to his death in the falls. His Indian sweetheart died and in his grief and sorrow, he went to join her by plunging over Shoshone Falls. The Idaho Power Company now has taken over the Falls for utility purposes and parts of the year the falls are nearly dry. The source of the company's power is Shoshone Falls. But they, too, have added to its attractiveness by lighting this great mass of water and during the season when it is back to its old glory, nothing is more enjoyable than a trip to the Falls in cool Idaho evenings, to view this tremendous cataract lighted. The floodlight structure is of concrete and is fastened to the face of the promontory of rock jutting out to the very water's edge and tied to cliff over the turbulent waters.

The first workmen were let down on ropes so that footings could be cut into the rock for the concrete foundations. Thirty floodlights with a combined capacity of 25,000,000-candle power are fastened to the steel frame of the structure. The lamps project a rectangular beam of light and the several beams are really joined together to give a uniform distribution and intensity of light. It is a breathtaking experience when one first gazes on these illuminated waters, colored like the rainbow. The cataract is between massive walls, rugged and wild. One hears that sullen roar, the black walls of the canyon are lost in the darkness and the waters above and below the falls are shaded—a haunting, lonely something engulfs you, then suddenly the lights are on! Then you gaze at the supreme loveliness of the scene before you. There, that huge back of living snow, foaming and gurgling and plunging over the precipice with a mighty roar, and it seems held there before your gaze, suspended without beginning or end, as it alone is visible.

One man describes it, "An ecstasy of brilliancy, a cascade of polished diamonds, a great derby of raindrops with mists rising like a cloud of fairy wedding veils." Then the final touch of glory is added—a tiny, but perfect rainbow—an arch of dream colors forming a true semi-circle on the rim of a mighty canyon. There is nothing that can approach the wonder and beauty of Shoshone Falls illuminated. It is the combining of grand Old Nature with the inventive ingenuity of man, by combining and harnessing this gigantic secret of the air (electricity) and using it to beautify one of the world's greatest elements—water.

Grace and I reveled in all this scenery and stupendous working of nature. We thought we had seen it all but Frank had proved us wrong by these camping trips we had all taken together.

Our rock house was soon to be finished and then we would be married, move in, and start ranching in Idaho. We had invited Grace to live with us but she had promised to tutor the young daughter of I.B. Perrine, the man we had been working for at his Blue Lakes Ranch. We also informed him that he must look for new teachers for the

Jerome school, which was being built over across the river in the little sagebrush town. Mother and Father were opposed to me marrying a man I knew so little about but I was unafraid and we felt we both were old enough to know what we were doing. Anyway, we were married in late summer.

We had lots of fun choosing our furniture and placing it. Our little home was very attractive, to us at least. Of course, the water had to be carried from a canal that they had put through our land for irrigation purposes. For our drinking water, we went to a spring down in the canyon a mile away and put it in a canvas water bag. That had to last us all day and as we had no shade, we just moved it around the sides of the house to keep it out of the sun. Everyone carried their drinking water in these canvas water bags, either kept them in their houses or shacks and when in the field, took it along and placed under a wagon or machinery to keep in the shade.

"We won't have a honeymoon just now, dear," said Frank. "We are rushed right now in the office but later on I'll take you to Portland, Seattle and on to Victoria in time for the races. You'll love them." I was very happy and right then didn't care if we ever had a honeymoon.

Grace did stay awhile with us and took charge of the cooking but I was learning to cook, too, and for the first time enjoyed a recipe book. Grace was a big help, but was a bit stubborn about changing her mind, especially about the food she cooked. If it pleased her, it was OK. And you just had to like the way she cooked it. Arguing with her was like trying to blow out an electric light bulb. But she was a true friend and pal. She was witty, too. One morning she asked me, "Do you like sheet music?"

"Why, yes, if it is my kind of music, why?" I replied.

"Oh, I mean SNORING!" said Grace, "Isn't that sheet music?"

I had learned to cook quite well before Grace left for her work at the Blue Lakes Ranch. Frank was trying to sell out his real estate business so he could be at home all of the time. This was good news to me for it was lonely with him away so much. We spent every spare moment now planning our landscaping. With pencil and paper, we outlined our yard and then proceeded to place trees, shrubs and flower beds. I loved flowers with a passion and Frank left the choice to me. He said his mother never had flowers and he didn't know one from another. We set out a small orchard trying to have fruit of all kinds; we also had berries of every kind that would grow in our area. It wasn't all easy though, for some would die and would have to be replaced over and over but we weren't discouraged.

Our first garden was a queer hodgepodge of everything run together. We made high beds of dirt as they did in the East for our lettuce, radishes and onions, never once thinking that it would be impossible to water them from irrigation ditches. Of course, that all had to be done over again. How happy Frank was when he found the first ripe strawberry, rushing in like a schoolboy, face aglow and hatless. It was the same with all the fruit. He came in one day with two pansies and said, "I even picked the first hollyhock." I didn't even smile for he had told me he didn't know one flower from another and I guess he didn't. He was later, though, to become a peony fancier and an authority, too, on their culture.

We were like two children with new toys and very, very happy. Our conversations were usually pasted together with sticky endearments, but, why not? Our affections had been bottled up for a very long time before we met each other. I used to wonder how people who had been married for many years could still find in each other excitement, love and patience. Now I knew that our love would grow along with the years and when we became old, we would still find the excitement, surprise and wonder in each other. I was right. My heart always beat a bit faster years later when I heard his footfall on the porch and the days sparkled always for us. We could and did dream our dreams as of old. Life is to be lived, consumed and enjoyed.

After we had our plantings made and our lawn seeded, Frank wanted to take our honeymoon trip. I packed a trunk and two suitcases. Think of it. When now we see just how lightly we can travel! Trunks are relegated to the attics, that is, if there are any in existence now.

We had friends who would look after the ranch, so we boarded the train at noon and one night out and a day and we were in Portland, a quaint and beautiful little city—not swollen by the hoards of people who at present make it their home. Every yard had its lovely roses. Many an old house was moss covered, which added so much to its old country charm. Frank had lived there sometime before and was very familiar with its worthwhile sites, its hotels and restaurants. He insisted that I try every kind of seafood. I was game until it came to eels and I rebelled. They reminded me so much of snakes. I know now that they are delicious. We dined and wined at every good restaurant in town and usually ended the day by indulging in a big platter of crawfish, accompanied always by a big bowl of water (finger bowl). We found out that we needed it very much. Frank was wonderful company.

Later we went to Seattle but after a day there we hurried to Victoria to the races. There we took an apartment.

There was a cute little cook stove in it and the landlady lost no time in instructing me that she wanted it rubbed with tallow every day and then polished. There were worlds of wood to burn as we were close to the big forests of the Island.

On our first trip to the races, we visited the barns and petted and sugared the trim running horses. We were watched closely, though, and in some stables we were not even permitted to enter. It was the first real races outside of the country fairs that I had ever attended and I enjoyed every minute. After we knew our horse better we placed a few bets and then, believe me, it was exciting! We always laughed and said, if we won, we would have a big feast for dinner and if we lost we would warm up what we had the day before.

We did sightseeing, too, in Victoria, and at that time it was a page out of old England—its old ivy covered castle, its English food, its streets and its people were so much like England. Of course, we rode in the tallyho, so high up that we had to have a small ladder to get in. Then we could see the spacious and well kept grounds of the many estates, surrounded by high walls. We walked through their forest, with ferns shoulder high and then on to the sea. Victoria was enchantingly lovely. After the races, we went to Vancouver where I had several relatives living. In the meantime, I had lost my trunk with all my pretty dresses and it was a month before it was located, even after we returned home.

We found our home intact but weeds nearly as high as the fences so back to work for us until we had it all in trim order again. We brought back many ideas as to landscaping and at once tried them out in our home. Our trees had grown a bit in the short lapse of time. I rather coveted and wished for the great trees in Victoria and the saucy little bubbling waterfalls around each bend, but one can't have everything and after all, Idaho was our home and it was a grand glorious state to live in.

Frank had found and bought me a lovely mare in Portland. She was jet black and had been retired from the tracks. She was the possessor of many blue ribbons and I was very proud of her. She was perfectly gentle. Later we bought a cow, (Her name was Cream) and a few chickens and a hog. Now we were ranchers proper. We both had to learn to irrigate and they say to be a good irrigator one must be able to make water run up hill. It was said that only a Mormon could do that. We had many Mormon settlers in our neighborhood and they were kind and obliging. We were invited to all the Mormon dances and were treated royally.

My brother Roy had married several years before I did and they were coming to make us a visit. We were looking forward to it. I was anxious to have them meet my wonderful husband and prove to them that I knew what I was doing when I chose him. Another month and they came. They, too, fell in love with Idaho and decided to go back to Iowa and sell out and move out to Idaho. That would be wonderful for me to have someone of my own. Mother and Father were thinking of coming out to live, too. They were alone now and quite lonely. Ray and Guy were in the sheep business in South Dakota.

Frank located a farm for Roy. They, too, had their problems adapting themselves to a ranch, as Roy had been in his blacksmith shop for years. But a year on the ranch and they were here to stay. I was proud when I made my first butter and learned to pack it in one-pound blocks and wrap it in paper with my name on it. I churned every other day. I had learned to bake good bread, too, and was proud of my skill turning out pies and cakes.

Wash days were hard yet as I washed like Mother used to for quite awhile. We carried the water from canals and, of course, scrubbed on a board and boiled just as Mother used to do. Later on Frank brought home a washer, one that had to be turned back and forth by hand. He would always do that so my washings became much easier.

We had been married three years when out our little daughter came to brighten our lives. We named her Kathleen. Was Frank a proud father! It rather changed our way of life as we had developed a certain routine as to work and play and now we found, especially me, that this little girl made a vast difference in our home life. Babies—of all growing things the most wonderful I think, are babies. Just a baby! They come to us out of the dusk of centuries—little mendicants of love, bringing from golden pools of mystery, laughter and song. Their little bodies drenched with sun—their hearts crystal goblets brimming with rich nectar for our lips to sip; their souls, lovely notes in tune with all the spheres. Creation's world flashed and trembled at their coming—a lovely combination of love, hope and faith—a wonderful trinity. In these little minds and bodies are mysteries of spirit and life yet to be defined. Minds yet to be developed with a slow sturdy growth that MUST and WILL solve the still unsolved problems. All the myriad accomplishments of the world are but the unfolding and growth of baby minds. Now our plans for the future, of course, centered around our baby, her education and her welfare.

When she was but one year old, Frank drove into our drive with a lovely child's surrey with side lamps and an exact copy of a regular surrey and hitched to it were a team of Welch ponies, a trifle larger than a Shetland. They were perfectly matched. I rushed out to find out what it was all about, "Why they are for Kathleen," he said.

"Why, Frank, she is but a year old," I answered.

"I know, but I want her to start young to learn to drive," replied Frank and she did. They were her favorite companions and playmates until they died of old age.

One day a wagon brought out a finished playhouse with built-ins and it had a place on our lawn. No child ever had more things to entertain her than Kathleen, but, she shared them all with her little friends and she grew up loving animals of all kinds. She had her dogs, cats and even a pet goat, as well as a canary, turtle, hen, a salamander and a pool of fish.

We did not start her to school until she was seven for she would have to go on a school wagon driven by horses and the roads were rough and rutted in the winter months. Later, of course, we had fine school buses.

Our home was growing into a showplace down through the years and we were very proud of it. This is what one woman saw in it and this was printed in the Salt Lake Tribune:

"The Wilson home, Dreamworld, is located about three miles from Twin Falls and they have made it one of the most homey and attractive homes in the state, not from a place already farmed, but from the raw sagebrush land. It has been their home for thirty-six years. The first time I visited them, I wanted to stay on for hours wandering through their various charming gardens. Everything fascinated me from the grass-banked lateral winding through the trees with a small boat ready for a row, the completely equipped playhouse for the daughter, a cozy tree seat near it.

Flowers and shrubs of all kinds grew in profusion. A few years after my first visit, a pool and summerhouse had been added, I thought then that Mrs. Wilson's garden had reached perfection and would be hard to make it more enticing, but not content, Mrs. Wilson and her daughter conceived and made another garden hidden away in a vine covered corner, the entrance to it, a rustic wooden door inscribed, "Garden of Yesterday." I was surprised and delighted when I entered beyond the door to find a miniature garden portraying the yesterdays of Idaho. A small log house with its fireplace and rail fence enclosing it was the center of attraction. A dog was sleeping beside a little old woman standing in the doorway, with her old fashioned calico dress and apron, a chicken or two, a sleeping cat and a pig supposedly eating from a trough and cattle nearby. There was, also, a well with rope and bucket attached, an old mill and a miniature wheel was spilling water over into a tiny river. It was fed by a large water wheel hidden in the shrubbery.

On a small road was a miniature covered wagon and nearby an Indian camp, wigwams, laid campfire and several Indians lying around. From there the garden turned into low hills ending in a small mountain in the rear where wild animals, mountain lion, buffalo, eagle and even a rattler coiled to strike. In all, there are about 100 miniature animals and birds in this little make-believe garden. Iva Wilson has written many a news item, trade journal articles and farm articles, short stories and poems, but among them all it would be impossible to find anything more fascinating than her, "Story of Yesterday," not written in words, but intangible material at had, aided by rain, sunshine and nature's unfailing guardianship. On this door to the garden are the words, "Where the quiet, colored end of evening smiles." Mrs. Wilson is a pioneer of miniature gardening in southern Idaho. Hundreds of people visit her gardens every year. They love its quiet and beauty, crude as it is. The tinkling music of the river, the drowsy splash of the water wheel adds to its appeal."

— This article was from the editor of the Salt Lake Tribune, Salt Lake City, Utah.

So you see, outside of our own deep satisfaction in creating our gardens, we added to the pleasure of many people. Beautifying your surroundings does really pay off, in the joy and pleasure you give to other folks. We had many notables visit our place, too. Madame Schumann—Heink, who furnished me with an interview for "*Everygirl's Magazine*", Harold Wright, Buffalo Bill who had his picture taken with our little daughter and others. I, also, had garden seeds and plants given me by famous people. Woodrow Wilson and Margaret sent me, "forget-me-not" seeds, Zane Grey, sagebrush, Harold Bell Wright, a rose bush and Marion Talley, a lilac and others I can't remember now.

Another one of our gardens we liked immensely was our, "Moonlight Garden." It was, of course, in a corner by itself. The flowers were all white roses, spirea, glads, pansies and all the white flowers that we could get that would grow in Idaho. A fence covered with the moon vine enclosed this garden. The effect on a moonlit night was mystic and very, very beautiful. Some of my friends thought it, "chilly" and depressing, but to us it was just a bit of fairyland.

Another garden we liked was our Dutch garden of tulips and daffodils—flowers with a place to put your nose and lots of little figures. There were the girls with a yoke across their shoulders carrying water, wooden shoes, the goose girl and, of course, windmills. In it, too, I had various pieces of furniture consisting of trimmed hedge, a large basket with a handle and two armchairs and a sofa. They were perfect in shape and from a distance, one would think they were real furniture. All our little gardens were separate and stood out by themselves, all giving one that wonderful sense of peace and quiet—as quiet as a turkey farm on a Thanksgiving afternoon. We had worlds of visitors and, of course, enjoyed sharing our home with them as far as we had time, although many a pie scorched in the oven or pots burned dry while I was out on the grounds with someone showing our precious little gardens.

We didn't work all of the time. We were both so interested in Idaho's past history that we made trips frequently to old, interesting places. Cars were beginning to come to our country but horse lovers as we were, we still used our horses for the road as well as on the ranch. Our horses were all-standard and did not know much about ranch work. I remember we had a small garden plow and Frank thought he would train my mare to pull it and save him a big hoeing job in our vegetable garden. But, she refused to budge as she didn't know what was required of her. He suggested I ride her and guide her along the rows of vegetables, so I sat astride of her and by coaxing and talking to her, she at last started up and tried to do her part ranching. I felt sorry for her, for a race cart or a buggy was more to her taste. But adaptation seemed to be the law of the land in Idaho for the majority of us.

Fishing was tops in Idaho and we went every now and then. We loaded up the buggy with what we would need overnight and started on a 20 mile trip to stock our larder with a few fish. I had learned to can them, too, so when we had a surplus I would slap them into the cans and then in the winter we could have our fish fries whenever we chose. Rock Creek was to be our destination. We made camp and I carried pine boughs for our bed while Frank dug a hole right in the middle of our supposed bed site. When I inquired what he was going to bury, he said, "You will be thankful for that hole before morning. Our hips will sink nicely through the pine boughs and not reach the hard unyielding earth." So I found out too, and we had a wonderful bed.

In the meantime, I had discovered we were close to the well-known Rock Creek Store, which is an old historical landmark. It was right up my alley, then, to visit this store and get all the historical data that I could although I was familiar with some of it. Most of the early days of Snake River Valley are woven around this building. It was the first trading post west of Fort Hall, in the midst of the Real West, where the Indians outnumbered the white man one hundred to one. It was here in the early 1860's that ruffians killed Hugh Qui so that they might start a graveyard. In this store many a time midnight oil was burned and cards were dealt for big stakes. Many travelers made weary and despondent by the dusty, tedious, dangerous travel over the Oregon Trail, were given a new lease on life by the hospitality, encouragement and service given to them at this store. It was here that early settlers came for miles around for their supplies and received them either with or without "script." It was here that glasses clinked and the cordial handshake sealed a friendship that lasted a lifetime. It was here that Buffalo Horn came with his warriors the day he started on his "massacre along the Snake."

Colorful characters, who are leaving one by one, admired and revered by the younger generation. They gave to us our Golden West—blazed the trail with such daring and fortitude that we might enjoy the advantages and returns of this land in comfort and peace. I came back to earth from my sojourn into Idaho's past and returned to camp. Frank was busy frying fish, lovely big trout. The fire was purring against a green log backstop, geese were yapping in the clear sky above us and a crane planed overhead. He looked up with that charming smile of his and said, "Just in time, my dear. The coffee is about ready."

My heart ganged up with my willful feet and I hurried to him for a big kiss on his cheek. "Gee, Frank, am I a piker to desert you but that darn store was too close to pass up."

"It is alright, I know your failing when history beckons. I have been there and I like it, too." We sat down by the river to feast on his labor. We sat where the river zipped yowling into the canyon. It was a lovely spot. No wonder the Indians fought the white man for it to the bitter end. I washed our few dishes and Frank went back to try his luck again. We couldn't stay too long these days for now we had Kathleen to think of. I always planned to be home when she returned from school or from Roy's where we had left her overnight. Time was slipping by and, at last, Frank with a fine catch again, was ready for home. As we followed the river, always, a mist arose and the river's night song seemed to be reduced to silent muttering. We just beat the storm a few minutes. Home again. I hated to leave the pine boughs behind, but our feather bed would feel mighty comfortable.

Julius Stindie says, "Where love has found a home, every new year forms one more ring around the hearts of those who love each other." This was certainly true of our dear little home. Entering it, I always think of the old Gaelic phrase, "My little share of the world." I want beauty everywhere in my home and I want it to breathe home atmosphere from every angle and I know it does. Our home seems to me to be thoroughly humanized for it has the deft little touches that make it different from any other home as does our outdoor landscaping—a home must have individuality, as well as charm and we feel that we have attained. We have no expensive Chippendale, Sheraton nor the tawny glory of Hepplo white with its exquisite inlay, but we do not miss it nor need it in our sweet little home. The qualifications of a true home, to me, are comfort, personality, homeliness and livability. Goethe says, "He is happiest be he king or peasant, who finds peace in his own home."

Up to this time, we had just had kerosene lamps but now the Power Company informed us that if we could interest three more neighbors who would sign up for electricity, they would build us a line from the main highway. We lost no time in interviewing our neighbor and succeeded in getting them signed up. The line was to be built at once. We had the house wired the year before for Delco lights, a system where we would generate our own lights. Now, if we installed the electricity, we would be able to even cook with electricity. I could hardly wait until the line was in and it was not long until it was a reality. I remember I went through the house turning on every bulb. How wonderful it was for us! The next day we went shopping for an electric range. Frank had bought me a very nice kerosene stove with a glass front in the oven and I was very proud of it. I loved to look through the glass door and watch my golden bread bake with a crust tinted just the right shade of gold. The Power Company sent out a woman to show me how to regulate the stove and how to use my oven. I remember a clock was supposed to be set at a certain time and food I had in the oven, if timed, could be turned off when it was done. I would put in a baked dinner; go to town and when we came home, our meal would be ready. Only one time the clock refused to start the oven and we came home cold and hungry, but when I opened the oven the food was in the same condition it was when I put it in... uncooked. But that only happened once. Other times, it was wonderful to come home to a cooked dinner, just set the table and presto! Our meal was ready, hot and steaming.

Now we had electricity, perhaps, later we could have a deep well and plumbing. So far, we had been using cistern water, which was better than carrying it from the canal and bringing the drinking water from the distant spring. We were careful to filter the water into the cistern and the result would be pure drinking water. We filled this cistern about twice a year. The water came in from a ditch and had to pass through very fine gravel, then through several layers of cotton baton and then through solid brick into the cistern so that everything foreign would be filtered out. Of course, it was a slow process, taking days and days for the water to trickle into the cistern through all of the filters, but we knew we were using pure water.

Now we wanted a well and had engaged a well driller to come. I had him to cook for and he was over a month drilling. He had gone down 180 feet before he found even a trickle. He said he'd go deep enough so we would be sure of having a steady and lasting flow and the result was a well better than three hundred feet. It was clear and cold but, oh, my it was hard, but it was the experience of all that had drilled wells. We had him case the well down the three hundred feet so that the irrigation water in after years couldn't come into our well.

Frank built a well house over the well and equipped it as a modern laundry. I had built-in tubs, a water heater and an electric washing machine. My washings were very easy after that. The next year, we installed a bathroom and had the water pumped into the house. We built a septic tank, too, and toilet so we had every convenience of a townhome. It seemed my happiness was complete. But with your own water system, there is always bound to be more or less trouble. It seemed we always had a pump man to repair the pump or locate a pipe that was leaking. Later on, though, with better mechanics and a knowledge ourselves of the workings of our own system, lots of this trouble was eliminated. I still struggled with the hard water problem. After a time, water softeners were placed on the market. We decided to install one. It was rather crude, nothing like the ones of today, but it did soften the water, but every ten days the softener had to be regenerated which meant turning several gadgets and leaving for a stipulated time and then draining off the saltwater. After an hour and ten minutes one was ready to turn on again for the freshened water. Every three months there had to be one hundred pounds of salt added to the tank. I dreaded the regenerating for it meant staying in the well house basement that long, turning gadgets and watching the clock, so many minutes for each different operation. But it was all in a day's work. It was tiresome, though, and when I emerged from that basement, I was like the little puppy whose tongue was hung out to dry.

Electricity and especially electric lights are a tremendous advantage from a standpoint of safety as they forever abolish the use of the dangerous lamp and lantern. It is safe even for children to operate. It is said that electricity requires "more brains to make and less brains to use than any other commodity." Every year we tried to improve a bit. Tchekhoff, the Russian writer, said, "If everyone did all he could on his piece of land, how beautiful our earth would be."

The next thing we had planned was a fish pool. I had always wanted one. I wanted goldfish and water lilies and a pool would be an answer to that one. We never put off doing things that we had planned—no chance for us to "cool off" so we immediately started. It was a large pool and it took days to dig. It had irregular lines curving in and out, gracefully spread out on our back lawn. We installed a fountain in the center and wired for underwater lighting. We cemented it, leaving a shell of cement about a foot from the top to put pots of water plants on. The rim we rocked with rocks from nearly every state in the U.S.A. that we had been collecting for a long time. In the yard, we also had a floodlight real near so its beams would light up the entire surface. How thrilled we were when we first turned on the lights. They attracted the bugs to the water and the fish had a feast. We had many little figures to enhance it like a small boat with a boy fishing bobbing around on its surface, a frog or two about to plunge in, a duck, two pelicans and many other little figures. On the rim, we had cut into the cement the words, "DROWSY WATER." Doing all the work ourselves on these different projects made the cost negligible. Our little gardens brought many visitors to our home and it was really getting to be a burden on our time, but I guess we had "asked for it." I was writing a bit, too, for farm papers, trade journals and boys' and girls' papers. All that took time also. The days just were not long enough.

Idaho's Historian

Idaho's historian had written a book on the early days (Indian Days) of Idaho and he requested that I typewrite it, a small book of perhaps 25,000 words. He was then nearly eighty and I just couldn't refuse him. It was a laborious task as his writing was very poor, but I got through somehow and now it is in nearly every library in Idaho. His name was Charles Walgamott and he is called Idaho's historian and is loved and remembered as such. His life as he said, "Has been one continuous panorama of moving pictures for a period of more than fifty years," and he has recorded them in the pages of history. History that will go down through generations as a true picture of the old Idaho in all its colorful past. May we be loyal and true to our heritage as our old historian is to his love—IDAHO. In nearly all these histories, he had participated. He said, "I loved the mountains, the mountain streams, western people with their hospitality and their western ways, the smoky odor of Indians tanning buckskin, so prevalent around the campfires intermingled with the smell of sage; the ever present element of risk and the frequent solitude which has its own fascination." Mr. Walgamott knew and loved Idaho when Indians skirted through the sagebrush; when men were quick with the six shooter, when roundups were the social affairs, when men decorated lonely cottonwoods with some, "law breaker," at a "necktie," party, when great herds crossed her valleys and when MEN were MEN. With him there lingered something of the old charm and romance of the past. His handclasp, his smile and a genuineness that is missing in most of us today. His eyes clear and bright, looked through you and passed you as though seeing again the scenes he loved and treasured. When he crossed the great divide into the boundless unknown out into the golden sunset, he left behind him these treasured stories of history that will be read and reread by the coming generations of Idaho's loyal citizens. May they always love and cherish their birthright with the same ardor as our grand old historian of our beloved Idaho, CHARLES SHIRLEY WALGAMOTT.

The Snake River Valley's First School

Here, I would like to describe the very first school in the South Snake River Valley, as told by Mrs. Hayes, the daughter of the first teacher. Quote, "A lusty voiced cowbell clanged out the call to classes in September, 1876. That cowbell may have had something of the same significance as had the famous bell which rang out at Independence Hall one hundred years before it too, was proclaiming liberty and equal opportunity for American children." The teacher was John Hansen, a native of Denmark, seeking health and fortune in this new land.

The stage line had been established in 1846 from Salt Lake City, Utah to The Dalles, in Oregon, but after the railroad was completed from Utah to the Pacific coast a much shorter route for the stage was located joining the old trail at Rock Creek Station in Idaho. In 1876, several settlers who had been working on the railroad had brought their families over the divide, where along the streams of clear and pure water, they made their new homes.

John Hansen, even in Denmark through letters, had heard of Idaho and its rich promise of hills and streams laden with gold and silver, so he came on a westbound train, came to this then faraway land. He stopped at the sagebrush station, never realizing that its mud–chinked walls would enclose the first school in this valley. He did not come to teach school, but there were seasons of unemployment as long ago as 1876 and when the meager harvests were over and the gold failed to materialize, he began to look for something else to do.

He found a home where there were several children and offered himself as a teacher. Equipped, as was the fashion for the 1876-model schoolteacher with Latin, mathematics, history, reading, writing and spelling, he got the job. A room at the station was secured at the schoolhouse. Grain and hay for the horses stored in one end of the room was covered over with burlap sacks.

Stranded travelers or extra "hands" were bedded down there at night, but for a short season by day, this dirt-roofed, dirt-floored room lured all the children in the valley between the ages of six and nineteen by the miracle of its learning. The teacher's desk was a goods box on which reposed one or two books, his one lead pencil, a few freshly cut willow sticks and the urgent voiced cowbell. There were eleven pupils, some of them walking, some riding horseback six or seven miles each day to and from school. They sat in two rows on backless benches, boys on one side and girls on the other, the short legs of the tiny ones dangling in space, the long legs of the tall boys sprawled over the dirt floor. Perhaps they wrote notes to each other, scratching the words out on the hardpack dirt floor, with the heel of a boot or the end of a willow. Possibly, however, willows had other uses in that long ago schoolroom. There was no blackboard for the schoolroom, but some of the pupils had slates and there were a few pencils and a very few pieces of brown wrapping paper for special written work.

Lessons were for the most part, oral, and penmanship was developed to the scratching rhythm of pencils on hard slate as the teacher counted, "One, up; two, down; three, up; four, down; "A." The few books used in that school were sent up from former neighbors in Utah, but the teacher was supposed to know enough to make books almost dispensable. There was no modern busy work for little hands to do and workbooks for any age but the little ones bent diligently to their sums on the borrowed slates, while the "big" class, owners of the slates, stood up in a row before the teacher to recite some lesson for which no slate was needed. Painstakingly, letter–by–letter, word–by–word, they learned the fascinating skill of reading. For the history lesson, the teacher read or told stories about America and other lands, then, later in the day, the pupils stood up and recited back to the teacher, as nearly as possible, what the teacher had spoken. There were only two classes, the "big class" and the "little class."

Although some of the pupils were indeed big, there was not much difference in the type of lesson provided for them. Some of the older children had been pioneering all their lives and had never before enjoyed a term of school. The few, who had learned to read, helped the others under the teacher's guidance. The teacher was a stern disciplinarian. Reared by a stern schoolmaster in a Danish school, no pupil even dared raise his eyes from his lesson book for fear of punishment. John exacted silent obedience to his every command. When written work was done, the pupils were expected to sit erect, with arms folded across their chest like stolid Indians. But when recess came, the teacher organized games on the narrow strip of meadow along the creek, playing hilariously with the big boys and helping the little ones to build their houses of sticks and stones or fashion dolls and whistles from the green willow sticks. At the end of every day, if the pupils had been good, there was a fascinating story from Hans Christian Anderson and the rich grace of that master of fantastic stories fell upon those pioneer children like a mantle of magic, transforming the long journey home into an adventure with the Ugly Duckling, The Constant Tin Soldier, The Darning Needle or The Tinder Box.

The teacher was paid by "subscription." Parents of the children and other interested landowners contributed what they were able and the teacher was expected to take part of his pay by boarding at the homes of his few patrons. The subscription school persisted for several years before public support made a regular term of school possible any place in the valley. Even then, its maximum length was usually three months in the year with the teacher still boarding around among his patrons.

Sometimes classes were taught in one room of a family home. The teacher, with the help of the older boys and their fathers, built a rude cabin, which they proudly called the schoolhouse. Almost invariably, such a schoolhouse wherever it was, became the center of social life, where the teacher led a song session or a generous-hearted fiddler kept gay feet skipping till the rooster in a distant barnyard warned that time had come for another day of work. preempt

Autumn came early here and the first chilly winds whining down from Goose Creek mountains, warned teacher and pupils alike that the heatless station school would have to be abandoned when winter came. One small window, a hole in the wall covered with oiled muslin let in a little light, but when the day was too cold for an open door the room was dark—so dark the teacher was obliged to light a candle. When the teacher thought that it was too cold for further teaching, the teacher would announce simply, "There will be no school tomorrow. This is the last day." Then without further remarks, he gave the customary command, "Stand. File out. March!" With usual silence, the children obeyed. When they were all outside, John, the teacher, stacked the four benches against the wall of the cabin, pushed the goods box back into a corner and with his books under his arm, set out to overtake the children, already straggling down the hard gravelly road. Thus ended the first term of school in the south Snake River Valley, in Idaho."

What a change there has been in schools in eighty-four years! But those little shack school rooms, as well as the later one room country schools, turned out some wonderful citizens, some world-renowned and thousands unknown, but yet, were the real salt of the earth. I taught many of those schools myself and I know whereof I speak.

Now back to my little home. We thought we were now very modern but my, how far we had yet to go to be as modern as today. Threshing time was here again and I had to do with that alone this year, but by now I liked to cook and loved to see the husky threshers stow away the food. The machinery had advanced from the horsepower of my childhood, but there were still the twenty-odd men to cook for and while I had electricity to cook with now, it still couldn't prepare all that bulk of food that would be consumed. So chickens were slaughtered, vegetables prepared, pies baked, rolls made and all the various other things that had to be done. When the day came, I was fully prepared for it and refused a kindly neighbor's offer to help, for I knew Frank would help me with the dishes and now, different from the old days, the men did go home to their suppers so one meal was all that was required. Another was the absence of the old fly switch that Roy and I had to wield over the men's heads while they were eating.

Yes, we had improved a bit here and there. Some of my neighbors were even taking the threshers into town to a restaurant for their noon meal, but somehow, we wanted to cook for them ourselves. I think I rather liked what the men said to other neighbors, "You sure get a feed at the Wilson's" and "Man, can she cook!" Yes, a bit conceited, I guess, but I liked it anyhow.

Frank had been drumming up another trip for us in his head and later proposed it to me. A trip up the "River of No Return." Idaho does have such a river and these days it is being done several times a year by adventurous folks. It was really dangerous in the old days but while full of thrills yet, it is not so dangerous. This river is the Middle Fork of the Salmon River, in the very heart of the wildest, most isolated and almost impenetrable country in Idaho. In places, the walls are so high that the riverbed is darkened. It flows through some of the grandest scenery in the world and man never saw some of it until a few years ago. Its swirling rapids are extremely dangerous. Wild animals are found in their native haunts in great numbers. Very few in those days ever had made the trip, only experts with boats and water. It is called, "The Trip of a Thousand Thrills."

The National Geographic Society with their usual daring made this trip down this treacherous river—a trip of three hundred and fifty miles, then taking twenty-three days in a twin-sculled barge. The trip was thrilling and several times only very skillful handling of the barge saved the company from the deadly rapids. They had but one mishap; the radio operator fell ill and died. He was taken out by airplane.

Much new geological data and the discovery of evidence of an ancient tribe of unidentified Indians was the result of the trip. Deep red pictures painted by the unknown tribe covered the rocky walls of the Salmon River Canyon. They were found almost the entire length of the river. The pictures seemed to relate tales of hunting. Men were pictured on some of the paintings and there is a kind of numbering system running into vertical lines. The paintings have been photographed and were studied by scientists. At that time, they took about four thousand pictures. The leaders of that trip said of this unexplored wilderness, that he had never made but one other journey that was more impressive and that was through India and the Himalayas.

As interesting and adventurous as was this trip, we decided not to take it. We had Kathleen to think of these days and the river would always be there with its mile-deep canyon. There were so many places out here in the west to go camping and have an outing besides these almost inaccessible and dangerous beauty spots. There is Yellowstone Park, only a day's drive with all its wonders and beauty, so familiar now to nearly everyone that I will not try to describe it. We made that trip twice. Then Lake Tahoe, incredible gem of the mountains, blue, cold, clear, twenty-one miles long and twelve miles wide, is set among the spectacular ridges of the Sierra Nevada, a breathtaking beauty spot. Utah, California and Arizona are all close neighbors these days with the car, and all of them possess such wonders, beauty spots and never-to-be forgotten camping spots, all historical and teeming with tales of the old West. What scenery is there to experience in the Grand Canyon and famous Bryce Canyon. So we never would lack for places to go without this one dangerous trip.

We liked music, both of us, and we had it in our home so that our child too would become music-conscious. I played the piano, Frank the "fiddle" and we had just bought a phonograph with twenty-five records, all the best music we could get. That, too, was a very luxurious piece of furniture and the afternoon we brought it home, we played the records over and over again and really forgot to eat our supper until time to retire. We had not heard of radio then. We had a few picture shows, and illustrated songs in the show houses. Grace was a good singer so she was engaged to sing the songs as the screen illustrated them. Of course, there were always the band concerts in the summertime in our new little park. These little "band stands" used to stand proudly in almost every town square back in Iowa. Here was the Sabbath's most exciting and about the only entertainment.

All of us, who came along before such new devices as movies, radio and television lured the folks indoors, can well remember when the warm breathe of summer, brought as surely as lilacs, the Sunday Band Concert. The soft wind rustled the leaves, old folks visited with neighbors, the youngsters played and scampered on the dandelion-dotted grass and lovers found seats in the shadows, where possibly, they might hold hands. The band leader in his uniform proudly brought down his baton and the familiar and glorious strains of Semper Fidelis bust forth or maybe "Ta-ra-ra-boom-der-e (a)." Even in this late day, our band still gives us one concert a week.

Some old customs still remain and I pray they always will. How we loved parades and it seemed that our town on the smallest pretext would stage a parade, old and young would all want to be in the parade. The circuses used to always have a parade, and how we all would get up before daylight and get everything done so that we might get into town and find us a good place where we could see it all. We used to take a sack with a bit of food, for often we had to stand hours before it started and did not dare to leave our place. We had one circus in Twin Falls that had a tragic ending. This was in the animal tent and we were all watching the keepers feed the animals when we heard a scream and a huge panther sprang through the air and grabbed a small child out of its mother's arms killing it as well as a Shetland pony before that. No one cared to see the circus that day.

Cars were getting now so numerous that we were almost forced to get one, as a horse and buggy was just about crowded into the ditch. We both wanted to keep driving horses but it wasn't pleasant anymore. Before the war came, we would hitch up our fastest horse and drive the three miles to town in the hopes we could find someone who wanted to race a mile or so and we always had a "taker". The roads were rough as we had no pavements then, but we enjoyed a good race and we always felt pretty sure of winning. There were quite a good number of very good "drivers" as we called the track–trained horses, in our town then.

Our first car was an Overland. Frank did not like cars and it was hard for him to learn to drive. Our first experience was a sorry one, too. We attempted to come down a steep grade and Frank had forgotten just what he was to do as he started down a grade and once on the way the car gained tremendous speed for those days and he just didn't know what to do to stop it or slow up. He just tried everything he could get ahold of that would move and luckily for us, he at last found what to do just before we came to a very dangerous curve. We were both frightened and when we did get the car stopped, we just sat there until someone else came along and towed us in.

The American Southwest

Frank was homesick for his real estate business again and hearing of a new country opening up in Texas, we decided to go there for a year and see what luck we would have again selling land to newcomers. By that time, Frank had driven a car quite a bit and we felt that we could make the trip by car. We hated to take Kathleen out of school but knew we could put her in the schools there and she wouldn't lose too much, if any, of her schoolwork. Texas schools were poor, though, at that time. We left our home in good hands and had no worry in that way. We started out one spring morning for the big state. Popcorn clouds hovered above us and the roadsides were steaming with spring.

This would be one part of the West and Southwest we had not seen with exception to Utah. We had toured that state pretty thoroughly and that part of the trip we expected to go right thru without extra side attractions that we usually sought. We really started out in a rain and asked ourselves if it were a bad or good omen. All the puddles in the road were busily collecting raindrops and the clouds were lowering in a pouting manner—the wind fumbling among the leaves of the roadside trees. We were comfortable with plenty of food and good camping equipment with a tent that fastened to one side of our car for sleeping quarters. We had a bed in the back seat for Kathleen to curl up in. Nothing like the wonderful equipment of today, but that time we had the best offered. No nice motor courts like now, but there were motor camps all along the way and one could always stop in them where wood was furnished for the cooking on old ranges picked up here and there. The campground and the fuel and stoves cost you 25 cents overnight. We had a two-burner oil stove with us for cooking and had to use it when we found it impossible to find a camp before darkness set in.

Many we met were on their way southwest and southeast even seeking something they could not find where they came from. With some it was health, some farmland, business opportunities, grazing or rangeland to start a new spread for themselves. I can't remember any of them just vacationing as the many travelers of today. All would not find perhaps that which they sought in the Southwest or Southeast, but I am sure they all found incomparable places in which to search. Of course, all had their deficiencies. I have wondered about the hundreds of folks we met and talked with, how many of them found what they sought—maybe, found riches other than those which they sought, and stayed in that promising land and became rich in actual living.

Our first night out, we camped near the admonishing finger of a church steeple. The wind shouldered against the sides of the car and tent and the water was chucking out of the hillside near us. Our tent kept out the rain and our camping equipment was satisfactory in every way. We enjoyed ham and eggs and the hash browned spuds. I had boiled a kettle full of them at home and felt they would keep for several days in the cool weather. We had brought plenty of canned fruit and vegetables that could be cooked in a hurry on the little oil stove. We retired feeling cozy, happy and looking forward to when we would be in Arizona and New Mexico, which we knew, would be interesting—two states but one area, Mexico Territory.

Before that it was a major part of a single province of the Spanish colonial empire and before that the range of the nomadic Navajos, Apaches, who roamed and raided it, and the Pueblos and Hopis and Zunis and Papagos, and Pima and Yumas, who dotted nearly every part of it through the prehistoric years with weathering remains of their stone and adobe homes. We entered with awe and a bit of superstition. Time had passed over it but the pattern of the past remained. No other part of the west is like it. History has made markings upon it and these are small, scattered lonely scratches on the surface of this huge indifferent land. Here is one land where man does not dominate, where modern civilization is only a spidery network clotted in the few cities and along the few highways between, where wilderness is often only a stone's throw from those highways or even from the cities. It is a land of great distances, rugged badlands, arroyos and washes in Arizona. A land ripped and torn by Nature into gulches and canyons. A land where much of the basic earth is bare. It is a land of infinite variety—in it, you find all the geographic zones. In hours you leave a well watered valley, go out on the bleak desert, climb long rolling knolls, enter wonderful grassland, climb up on the mountain and to the timberline up to the lichen covered rocks and when you have climbed the highest peak, you find the eternal cold of the Arctic. Then from that peak, you look down into the desert stretching away past vision, tying the region together as one great whole.

The Indians found it thousands of years ago, the Spaniards, four hundred years ago and we Americans are finding it now. It is a land of Natural Wonders, lavish beyond any other region. Grand Canyon, Carlsbad Caverns, Petrified Forest, Painted Desert, White Sands, Sunset Crater, Organ Pipe, Cliff Dwellers Homes and the Saguaro cactus forest. It is a place where nature has played artist on a grand scale through all the mysterious ages. It is a land of sunlight and limitless space in which the earth lies poised. Sunlight there is a living presence, more of it and far purer then either California or Florida can produce. Part of these two states they claim, has sunlight eighty percent of the daylight hours in the year. It is a "magic mantle over the land during the day; a miracle of luminance on the ridges and far mountains in late afternoon, a superb always—different panorama of color in the evening setting—" are the words used by someone describing the sunset there. There is color everywhere in this vast witching land, which holds history in its huge protecting hand.

Its climate high and dry protects and reserves relics of the distant past and the poverty of its resources permits the past to live on. Man's very beginnings can be traced back to her—that is Man's beginnings in North America. This is the oldest and the youngest part of our country because here have been found the remains of the oldest civilization in the new world. Here it is claimed that the aboriginal had already developed a culture we still have, when the countries of Europe, were just birthing. This land knew Folsom and Cochise cultures fifteen thousand years ago.

Its deficiency is its lack of water, which preserves it from outside intrusion in a big commercial venture. Water would bring the plow, its skies would shrink to the overcast of moisture area, wilderness would give way to settlement and the sun would lose much of its golden glory, so its very poverty protects its allure and treasures. But there is also the harsh brutal beauty of sand storms, bitter winds and bitterer winter.

What we planned to see and what we did see was a visit to the Cliff Dweller homes of that long, long ago. On hollowed ledges of those towering cliffs are the ruins of the people who lived there in successive periods, more than four hundred prehistoric sites and 140 major sites just in one canyon. The best known of these is the White House. It is claimed that it once contained one hundred and seventy-five rooms; three stories are still to be seen. It is plastered with white clay. They told us that this house was started about the time William the Conqueror invaded England. The Hopis lived here adding to it about the time Shakespeare wrote his plays, then came the Navajos who fought here to keep away the white man.

On the cliffs are painted Spanish soldiers riding across the rocks. Bones lie on the upper ledge of Navajo women and children slaughtered by Spanish soldiers; Kit Carson was the man who forced the final surrender of the Navajos. Navajos still roam through here with their flocks, they love their land even if they have so little. They live in dreams and remembrances of the recurrent tides of history.

Take any road, any trail, or hike and you will run into natural wonders everywhere. There are ancient ruins all over the area. Unknown ruins are being turned up by highway construction. Every area seems to have been a home site for some historic people. In northeast Arizona there are three ancient cave pueblos. Timbers imbedded in their roof indicate that these houses were constructed about 1243 A.D. Ventana Cave yields relics ranging from Folsom Man, about eight thousand years B.C., to modern Indian. It shows that it was continuously inhabited for ten thousand years. A trail leading to some of these cliff dwellers, supposed to be over six hundred years old, is still used by people getting to these houses. It is worn knee deep.

We could spend months and months here, but we were headed for the Lone Star state and felt we must be on our way. The lure of Arizona would call us back someday. New Mexico was interesting, too, with all the weirdness and a historic past rich in tradition. Santa Fe intrigued us, the City of the Holy Faith. It is the capital and, of course, a cosmopolitan city but there lingered the flavor of a small town. It has historical zones to protect itself against too much encroachment of modern construction.

Here we rubbed elbows with Indian, Spanish, artists, writers, historians, archaeologists, anthropologists and tourists. New Mexico has, also, a trackless waste of land, which someday may produce a now unknown mineral, or oil or what have you. It is a savage country, savage heat, savage dust and savage winds. It was nearly nightfall when we crossed the line and were in then, our largest state, Texas. The darkness was a soft blanket quilted with stars. We stopped when we came to the first small town so we might see Western Texas by daylight and then the roads were strange. We made early starts mornings and stopped early, too. Little spirals of dust were creeping along the curb like ghosts and there were small town street lights, beaming dimly at each other, trying to stay awake. I thought everything in Texas was BIG but the caretaker of the motor camp was a man so small he was really a waste of skin. He located us on the very outskirts of the camp. He was very smiling and accommodating, carrying us an armload of wood and offering to light the fire in the old rusty stove. "And this is Texas," piped Kathleen.

"Just the start, we have days of driving ahead," replied her Daddy.

Texas is certainly a region of superlatives, in a university, I saw the largest collection of mystery stories in existence, the deepest hole in Pecos County; the ugliest man I ever saw, features with a worn distinction like a head on an old coin; and the biggest hats on the men I ever saw, the tallest men and the biggest feet I ever saw on the postmaster of this little town. When I say Texas, I remember the mission bells, the millionaires in every hotel, the bootblacks with huge gray Stetsons (in Dallas), cowboys singing all night long near where we camped at Ft. Worth, the king-sized cigarettes they smoked and the largest St. Bernard dogs. I had thought of Texas as one big plain but western Texas was all bumps, bumps large enough to be termed mountains by the natives. It had its share of rocks, too, and waste barren land to buy, my, oh my, what has been found under that land—black gold—oil and more oil. Texas certainly spewed up its riches.

But San Antonio was the city that appealed to all of us. It's an old Spanish City real enough with a flower in its hair and a guitar in its hands. The narrow river meanders through the town like the stream of people, doubling on itself, turning up at unexpected places. Here in this ancient American city the brush–country, Texan momentarily forgot about the miles of mesquite and the endless plain. Adobe huts two hundred years old and more crouched in the shadow of skyscrapers. Blood and bravery, beauty, the terror and the glory of the human spirit were written in the curving streets. They had been trails stamped out by the feet of the Conquistadors, of the padres and the early Spanish settlers. And by the hoof of the Castilian cattle brought in by the Spaniards in 1690. Their wild offspring caught and bred and bred again through the centuries to Long Horns, Shorthorns and down to the present Brahmans of the present time.

No city in America has greater historic charm than San Antonio. Her ancient missions, mute tributes to Christianity in the wilderness, her Alamo Shrine of Texas liberty, her cow trails up which the herds of longhorns moved in the dim twilight of the yesterdays, her wagon roads, now beautiful paved streets, over which the prairie schooners creaked and teams of oxen sweated in the long ago; her rock fortresses where United States cavalrymen held the Indians at bay and protected the settlers in the Indian wars—these and countless other reminders of a wonderful past, cast an enchantment over this old, yet new city, not to be found anyplace else.

The very beginning of San Antonio's romantic history is entwined with that of Spain. From that beginning until now, even in the awkward stage when the straggling cow town was undergoing its transition into a city, San Antonio has savored of the Spanish influence. Everywhere its quaint charm has been talked of until there scarcely remains an American who has not determined someday, to visit bewitching old San Antonio. In San Antonio, at one time or another, all the great figures in the history of Texas have lived and linked her indelibly with their achievements. Here the flag of six different governments were unfurled until at last, Old Glory floated to the breeze, never to be lowered by hostile hands.

Here is the Sacred Alamo, where immortal Travis and his heroic band, consecrated the townsite of San Antonio with their blood, shed for liberty. When the first conquistadors came to San Antonio more than two centuries ago, they found at San Pedro Springs, now the heart of the lovely city park, the council grounds for the Indian tribes that inhabited the Southwest. Here, Spain set up her government and her councils met in convention for one hundred years. In pioneer days, the cowmen, the prospector, the trail driver, the home seeker, gathered. Here Theodore Roosevelt organized his famous Rough Riders. Here a full division that won distinction in the world war, was trained and equipped for service overseas.

San Antonio, too, is famous for its parks and playgrounds, 1100 acres of parks and for sheer natural beauty and attractive creative effect; no single spot in all San Antonio excels her Japanese Tea Garden. Beneath the hazy blue of Southern skies, a bit of far off Japan has been transplanted here. Nothing has been spared to give the tea garden a true Oriental atmosphere.

Among other historic sites and mementos of pioneer days, the old mill dam is a sight of never failing interest. It was there that pioneer Antonians brought corn to be ground into meal. Then the mission's people came from all over the world to revel in the mysteries of these aged landmarks of Christianity. Imagination carries one back a century ago or more, when the old bells at vesper time, rang with silvery tones that echoed up and down the peaceful valley and far off to the outlying hills—of candles that gleamed on the old stone altars and the voices of priests and people singing the benediction hymns.

Here, also, is still the Roman arched aqueduct and rock dam constructed by the Spaniards more than two centuries ago and part of a great irrigation system remains intact and reveals that the origin of San Antonio was due to agriculture. Here was the birthplace of irrigated farming. Fort Sam Houston, the historic military post is here and the world's greatest flying field is here. The Alamo! San Antonio is its home. As you stand in that shrine, you view with feelings that words cannot describe as you see proof of the mad glorious courage of a handful of men against a horde, men who had come from the East to this Texas wilderness to conquer and then to die. In the glass cases are the famed long rifles that had barked so hopelessly against the oncoming enemy. And there was the slashing knife of Bowie on his cot in the crumbling Alamo fortress. Bowie already dying of typhoid and pneumonia, wielding knife and pistol from his cot bed until they ran him through with their bayonets and it was finished. There at the far end of the dim room were the six flags that had flown over this land in sovereign authority—France, Spain, Mexico, The Republic of Texas, The Southern Confederacy and the United States.

Two hundred and fifty years of violence, struggle and unrest. Men dying, men fighting in buckskin, men attacking and at last the brave American rising in victory. Even when about to die, these men faced their adversary with fortitude and resolve, such was the early American.

All in all, San Antonio is a city never to be forgotten. Her people are happy; birds are singing and her people—

languid and content in the beauty and romance of it all. We could not linger longer for we must be on our way to Rio Grande Valley with its promise of a real estate boom. Our town was to be McAllen where all around citrus groves were being planted by the hundreds of acres. It was an irrigated country and easterners from Iowa, Kansas, Nebraska and Missouri were flocking in.

We arrived late one afternoon and located in a short time where there were housekeeping cabins, the first we had seen along the route. We had three rooms and were soon very comfortable. This might be our home for several months.

The car had come through with flying colors, though with some badly worn tires. We had but minor troubles all the way.

Our cabin was roughly built—each plank in it had something to say, scolding with every step. But we would make it homelike later. Darkness drifted to the rooms and piled up in the corners before we could get unloaded and our plunder placed and supper ready. Were we famished! In a few days, Kathleen was in school and Frank teamed up with an acquaintance in real estate. We found out, though, that a very large real estate firm was operating on a big scale—they brought in trainloads of people, and took them at once to a big enclosed boarding house where they were not able to contact the town folk. A high fence surrounded the boarding house and entertainment was provided for the guests. There was no bus service to the town as the boarding house was in the country a ways. They were taken out, also, in company cars and were not turned loose until they had bought and signed on the dotted line. Exorbitant prices were paid for this land. They took them to farms where they had stooges hired to tell them what tremendous crops were raised there in the valley. That was the organization that we had to contest. We did contact a few but could readily see that we could not make any big money as we did in the days when Twin Falls was being settled.

We took many trips over into Old Mexico as we were but a few miles from the border. We also spent many Sundays on the Gulf Coast. Kathleen and I loved to go to Point Isabel, the very point of Texas. We climbed to the top of an old lighthouse that had been deserted for many years as the harbor there had filled in so much that ships could not enter anymore. They have since dredged it. There are many points of interest in that part of Texas but nothing to compare with the San Antonio country.

We visited the famous King Ranch, whose beginnings and history would make a book of itself. All Texans were proud of their state and one old soldier told me he wished it could be fenced so high that no Yankee could ever get in. "We are a world of our own and can live without any other section of the world," he boastfully said to me.

We stayed six months and by that time were homesick for Idaho and there was not enough business to justify us in staying, so one sunny morning we turned the old car's nose homeward. Our trip home was uneventful. We met many nice people and took a different route going than we did in coming, we saw some new and, of course, beautiful scenery. Kathleen was very glad to get back to her schoolmates and her own school. Texas schools did not at that time measure up to Idaho. Kathleen was pretty loyal to her Idaho and Texas did not impress her as it did Frank and me.

Here is her description of a Texas town—*A Town on the Rio Grande*—"Squat buildings sprawled along the street in an effort to create an impression of magnitude and of bustling prosperity, but failed miserably in the attempt. Dust, palm fronds, orange skins, banana peels, choked the gutters. The paper in the rubbish, strewn in doorways of the stores, shifted listless with the fitful panting of the breeze. In the streaked and dusty windows, flyspecked posters announced some event of months ago. Wretched mongrels lay upon the sidewalks with complete resignation, tolerating the presence of an ever–increasing population of fleas. Against the dirty fronts of the buildings, ragged little bootblacks squatted disconsolately in doorways and waited for a customer who never appeared. Here and there palm leaves of a sickly green had drooped from the weight of their straggling withered branches. Against the wall were a few stunted banana plants, appearing harmless, but sheltering at the base of their leaves, the spidery black tarantula on a vacant lot, a snake slithered through the parched grass. Only a faint undulation of the ragged blades marked his passing. In the infinite blue void above, the Texas sun glared upon the puny beings who had invaded the land of the sluggish Rio Grande and the snake infested jungle of thorns." By Kathleen Wilson—age 14.

CHAPTER V

New Adventures

(1926 On-ward)

———— ◆ ————

O nce more we were happy to see our little home and our friends. Days sped by very quickly—time does when one is busy and we were certainly busy. Then the time came when Kathleen was in her senior year at school and we were planning and deciding what the program was after that. Mother had died during these last years. Father stayed with us most of the time. He was lonely and lost without Mother. He had depended so much on her always it seemed. But spring was here again and it was a time to start all over again—that is the way it seemed to me every spring. Everything took on new life and so should people, I guess, though spring really belongs to youth with its promise of richer things to come, the dream we want to come true, the ambitions to be realized. In the spring, we think of the resurrection of all Nature, the return to life of all dormant things—the mating of the earth with the seeds, the rebirth of the flowers and the mating call of all wildlife. Old folks love spring, too, but often it means looking back at the shadows of the yesteryears and all along the trail are mounds of buried hopes, ideals and ambitions and yet, spring gives the old, new hopes and ambitions, too. It is meant to do just that. Poetry and spring are inseparable. Both express the thoughts, passions and insight of the human soul—an outward expression of inward loveliness. When poetry and spring are in your soul, a tree is turned into a moonlight trysting place, a bird becomes a winged goddess, a pool of water, nondescript to the common eye, becomes a shimmering sliver of film reflecting gleaming pictures from the pages of life. Sidney Lanier has said, "Soul and nature of essence and form, reveals with wonderful force how these two have new and thrilling contacts and will adorn and complement each other. Soul and spirit need form and find it in nature, which IS formal. Nature needs life and finds it in spirit which is life giving." Spring and poetry play upon your heartstrings a chord of memory. They call for you the call of the lark, the whirr of the hummingbird, the laughter of the ocean, the song of the seashell. They capture for you the silence of the great desert and even the call of the coyote.

You hear the sob of the pine trees, the sigh of the nightingale and the secret of the stars and the purple mountaintops. Isn't there both spring and poetry in the breath of the daffodils, the perfume of the apple blossoms and the scent of fresh rain? Both bring visions of the future and dreams of the past. From such things are poems made and from such things are the fountains of your life, things that touch both the old and the young alike.

Graduation day came at last. We were very proud of Kathleen as all parents are, but she had made a record for our High School. During her last four years, she had been an "A" student. When it was all over, we took her for a short vacation to Yellowstone Park. We all enjoyed its wonders and beauty with which most of America is familiar so I won't go into detailed description of it. The bears came in for their share of attention but we gave them a wide berth as a nurse from Twin Falls had been killed by one of them the year before. We enjoyed as much as anything the miles of forest we had come through as we never tired of the majesty of the trees.

Later we decided on Kathleen going to a Junior college for two years and then to try and make Stanford University in Palo Alto, California. Our college was located in Pocatello, Idaho, less than two hundred miles away. That fall she was admitted. She was the most homesick mortal I ever saw. We managed to visit her every week or bring her home for weekends that whole first year. She had never been away from home before and we had all been so close to each other. The school was thorough and she made a remarkable record. The next year wasn't so bad for her but we managed to have her with us often.

She had decided on teaching and had majored in Spanish. She liked languages. The last part of the last year, she took the entrance examination for Stanford University.

At that time, they would admit but five hundred girls and that meant their grades had to be the best as well as background and character. It was weeks before we heard the result of her examination. She was on edge most of the time, so afraid she could not get in and then one day it happened. She was notified she had "made" it. We were all so glad for her. It seemed now that we had lost our girl, she would never be at home again as she was before but that is one of the sad things about being parents. Of course, one doesn't want them to stagnate without a plan for the future, but it is hard to see them grow up and away from loving arms and hearts. Her schoolmates were proud of her too, as she was the only one who passed the test. Of course, they take all the girls that they can find room for. The requirements are not so stiff. It is a wonderful university and its graduates have no trouble in securing good positions when they have finished there. She and I, for the rest of the summer after her graduation at Pocatello, were busy planning clothes and room requirements. A trunk now was necessary as she could not be home every week or so. Holidays were all that she could count on to come home through the year. The day came all too soon when she had to leave for California. We just felt that we could not let her go. But one can and does.

Frank now thought that I should have a "hobby" of some sort outside of my flowers, fancy work and the home. He said it would only be a short time before Kathleen would be out for herself and we would find ourselves really alone for the rest of our lives. He suggested that I take up writings as I had been writing a few farm articles for farm papers now and then. I thought about it a long time and at last thought, I would try trade journal writing as it seemed the easiest to me and, of course, keep on with my farm articles, the thing I knew the most about. I liked it from the first and did quite well with it.

From this, I branched off on the juveniles, articles and short stories and a few poems. It took up my time all right. I had one magazine, some girl's magazines not being published now, *Everygirl's*, I am sure, wanted a write-up or interview about some celebrity each month and so I attempted that. My first interview was with Madame Schumann-Heink. I was very nervous and a bit shaky as I approached her to ask for an interview. I must say she was very gracious and gave me the information I wanted and also gave me three pictures of her to use. Was I happy? The magazine took it and asked for more.

Buffalo Bill was my next victim. My husband knew Bill Cody a little through their mutual love of horses and that interview was easy, ending up with him wanting his picture with Kathleen. She had her picture with him years before when she was small, sitting on his lap.

I was then successful in contacting Marion Talley, then singing on Metropolitan, their youngest singer. She was so homey and a lovely person to contact.

Harold Belle Wright followed and then my last celebrity was Richard Haliburton. He was to lecture at our town and the B.P.W. Club were planning a big dinner for him just before his talk. I knew there would be no chance to interview him unless I could find a way to see him before the club did. I planned to board his train 40 miles away as he stopped at the last little station coming into our town. Frank drove me there in plenty of time and left me on my own. I had heard he was hard to contact and was a bit "smug" but I intended to try anyway, so when his train stopped for a short time at the little station, I boldly boarded the train (he had a private car) and asked the conductor to take me to him as I had an appointment (one-sided, however). I was let in and there were but two young men in the car, so I approached one who told me he was Haliburton's secretary and pointed out R. Haliburton in the very back seat. I approached timidly and he arose at once and asked me what he could do for me and I replied, "First, I am scared "pink" but I write for a magazine who asked me to get an interview and I would like a few notes about you, your life and your writing." He was gallantry itself and asked me to be seated and offered me candy he had beside him. Then he proceeded to give me the information I wanted and gave me two tickets for the talk that night and asked me to dine with him, too. I had to inform him that he was being met by this female contingent and would banquet with them.

When the train pulled into our little station, they were there to meet him and so was Frank to meet me. I was a bit "cocky" as Richard Haliburton assisted me out of the train and shook hands with me before the gaping and wondering B.P.W's. I still have his signature, dated with the additional words "enroute on train to Twin Falls."

Most celebrities are so human and down-to-earth. I had forgotten Zane Grey, a lovable chap. So my life was full, too, for my home and Frank came first and that entailed lots of work and many, many happy hours. I had nice neighbors, but they too, were busy and not very much visiting was done these days, not like the first days in this new country. My nearest neighbor was a scream and kept me entertained when I was with her. She was so scatter-brained that she never knew which foot she had in her mouth, but you can be assured she DID always have one anyway and her husband, as Frank said, "He talks for hours without mentioning just what he is talking about. If there IS a thought in his head, it is in solitary confinement." But, they were fine neighbors at that.

Kathleen wrote us once a week and her letters were full of her work, she loved Stanford and had won a six hundred dollar scholarship for the next year that would help out a lot, as college expenses do add up. The year slipped by with the short visits at Christmas time and early spring. One more year and she would have her Bachelor's Degree.

In the meantime, Frank's father and brother had died. Our families were thinning out. Then came the sad news that Guy, my baby brother had died suddenly. He lived in South Dakota and his wife wanted me to come visit. She said so many changes had taken place there and that it wasn't as it used to be. South Dakota was never as new, wild and woolly as North Dakota, but progress strides steadily through the Dakotas but often its steps are small. Sheepherders can now spend all summer on the range, snug in the comforts in their mobile homes and ranchers can round up their herds by plane and car. There were now two types of cowboys, one yet with cowboy boots and wide-brimmed hats yet in evidence but the majority are the drugstore type produced for the tourist trade.

Now a colossal monument looked down from the crags of Mt. Rushmore, deep in the Black Hills, where the granite faces of four great presidents—Washington, Lincoln, Jefferson and the first Roosevelt, gaze with symbolic vision over Dakota where still remain the true cowboys, usually faces battered and worn from years of weather and work. I look back to my days in Dakota, seeing the sodbusters, the fiddle-footed and the restless always settling, but never settled, those who would move back or move on, leaving shacks to weather away in the endless wind, the land grabbers who would preempt and homestead just long enough to prove up a title and sell out. Then the solid whipcord men, who would stand stubbornly through the hard years and their women who would stay and make homes seemingly lost, yet held in the immensity of the land. I can see them in memory; Finns, Russians, Germans, Scandinavians, Dutch, Irish and, yes, English. They came and came and the Dakotas wanted them and welcomed them.

They came as word spread that in Dakota the land was level with no trees nor brush to clear away. During one week, eight thousand ticketed from Chicago. Of course, when the drought years came, the land boom dwindled and many left but the whipcords stayed. That was Dakota and is Dakota, the real, enduring Dakota I knew. Guy had braved a lot of hardships to get his sheep ranch started but now he was gone.

I returned home saddened by my loss. Frank was glad to see me and for supper that night he wanted biscuits, so I made them for him, biscuits as "light as a baby's conscience," he always said. Before we were aware of time, Kathleen once again had finished her year, with her degree. She wanted very much to go another year and get her Master's Degree but hated to have us spend more money but again she had her scholarship and we insisted that she go on and we would manage. So she embarked on another year. That soon passed, too, and now our "baby" had graduated from Stanford University with a Bachelor's and Master's Degree and she graduated cum laude, too. We were happy parents. Before she came home she was engaged to teach in a high school in California, so her year's work was all planned before she came home. She wanted no vacation only to stay at home and work outdoors in her beloved gardens. She loved her animals of which she had quite a collection. Her little ponies had died long since, but she had a riding pony now, besides all the farm animals were her pets. So went a pleasant and remembered summer. Life jogged on for Frank and I both happy in our home and in our work.

After Kathleen started teaching, I sensed some way that she did not care for it, but she taught the two years and resigned. She had always planned a trip to Old Mexico and now insisted that I go, too. Her father did not want to go and he, too, insisted that I take this trip with Kathleen. We planned to be away for three weeks. She had contacted a friend and schoolmate who was engaged in social work and Kathleen became very much interested and decided to prepare herself for that work when we would return from Old Mexico.

Old Mexico

"*Bienvenidos amigos!*" That means welcome friends, down in historic Mexico where the welcome never ends. When Kathleen and I went to Mexico it had not seen many American tourists and I think we were welcome more heartily than perhaps they do today. Mexico has made almost magic progress in the last twenty-five years. We crossed the border at Nogales where our money was changed into pesos and then boarded our train. Our "grips" and handbag were sealed until we were in Mexico fifty miles. Our train was old and worn—we were told later that Mexico had bought old coaches from the United States that had been discarded. We traveled slowly and their roadbeds were certainly rough. There were just three of us in our coach for nearly two days, ourselves and a gentleman from Portland, a teacher on vacation. Our coach was kept locked and when we would stop at a station two soldiers always stood at the entrance. It seems that during their revolutions (which were many) trains going through their jungles lands had been attacked so soldiers still rode on all trains. Our meals were served on a little table placed in front of our seats and was cooked in one corner of the coach. The two men who looked after our car were both very courteous, almost servile in their attention. At every station we were met by crowds of folks, women with food, burro milk, goat milk and tortillas and on the other coaches, all Mexicans, ordered and were fed from their open windows. Pigs and dogs also were much in evidence, and before the train could start again, the conductor would first "shoo" all the pigs from under the train.

We stopped at Mazatlan overnight. It was a lovely beach and on the beach was a good hotel. The clerk met us with a handshake as if he were welcoming old friends. We had a comfortable room. I was famished but learned that they never served dinner before eight o'clock so we wandered to a small garden, opening from the lobby. It was a jungle of palms, banana trees and lots of exotic plants. We had been informed that the hotel had a giant snake, python I think, that roamed or slithered rather all over the place to kill rats and other unwanted visitors that seemed to be in all beach hotels and other buildings. Upon inquiry, we were told that it was taking its nap in among the shrubbery where we now sat. I was anxious to see it, but Kathleen said she had lost no snakes and did not want to see the monster. I insisted until a Mexican boy led me to the spot where it was enjoying its siesta. It certainly was big—like ones you see in a circus. Its colors were very beautiful. He told me when it awakened they would feed it young pigs, kittens or chickens and they must be alive, as it never ate any other kind of food. I certainly refused to see the feeding stunt.

The hotel had ramps instead of stairs so it could slither from one story to another. When we retired, Kathleen closed all the transoms and said she preferred the rats. The town was very colorful with a wonderful view of the ocean. We met a few Americans staying there who were interested in mining. Movie stars came there occasionally to make pictures. Beggars seemed to be everywhere in Mexico and we saw them here, too, in this first class hotel—little boys who would watch their chance to get in and then beg from the guests. One of the help, a janitor maybe, wielded a fierce looking bullwhip, to drive them out of the lobby. It made me shudder when it cut into their little bare legs.

We were usually awakened mornings, while we were in Mexico, by a burro honking his complaint about the nature of his existence. Poor little fellows. One sees them everywhere, bringing in wood from the hills, loaded down so that about all you see are its tiny hoofs and big ears. Mexicans are never in a hurry. While on the "slow train" to Mexico City, we were caught in the jungle at night by a terrific thunderstorm. I don't think I ever saw so much lightning nor heard the thunder peal out its anger more fiercely than that night; they just stopped the train and stayed in that sweltering jungle until morning. I guess it was the wise thing to do as the conductor said that often miles of road would be washed out and it was dangerous to attempt it.

But Mexico City was worth all the inconveniences of travel to reach it. The sky-high metropolis of Mexico boasted a million people when we were there, but now I am told that four and one half million people live there today. Even then it was an unforgettable blending of the ancient and the new, Chapultepec Castle, National Palace, Gardens of Xochimilco and the Pyramids. Chapultepec Park, once the favorite resort of Aztec Emperors—the castle which is the "White House" of Mexico and the gardens which date back many hundreds of years, the magnificent Cathedral. The story of Maximilian and Carlotta was made more real by seeing their furniture, their silver and the rooms where they had actually lived. Here on the Hill of Bells, Maximilian of Austria, blond, homesick and good and well intentioned closed one of the many sad and shuffled chapters of Mexican history.

We took the ride in the Gardens of Xochimilco. We drifted along leisurely to the guitar and mandolin music and soft musical voices of the Mexicans who in another boat glided softly beside us down those quiet waters. Flower girls, too, passed us in boats throwing to us a lovely bunch of flowers. We ate our meals at Sanborn's, operated by an American and had delicious food there, too. His restaurant was known as the House of Titles and belonged to a nobleman over six hundred years ago. We were rooming at the hotel Oregon, which, too, several hundred years ago had been the castle of royalty. We also attended their theatre, a wonderful building and at that time, had the only glass stage curtain known.

The University of Mexico was founded four centuries ago and is the oldest in North America. It is a few miles outside the city. The neural in high relief by Siqueiros, the wonderful library by O'Gorman, first in the world to be surfaced entirely by mosaics, shows just how Mexico has made in art and mind. We climbed their pyramid, too. The city itself is high and when you climb those high pyramids, you are really short of breath. I forget the measurements of the one we climbed, Pyramid of the Sun, if I remember rightly, something like three or four acres and perhaps more, it covered. Those huge stones were fitted in place perfectly, lifted by man himself, and the cement work so perfect that it does not have a crack after centuries and centuries. Their secret of the making has never been discovered yet.

On the very top of our pyramid that we climbed was a sacrificial alter and we were told that the sacrificed had to climb those steps and at the top the heart was taken out as a sacrifice. All along for miles, they were unearthing new pyramids and statues and concrete huge snakes, their smiling snake. Museums in the city were filled with all these strange figures. They then were excavating under these pyramids and were still unearthing another civilization even built before the pyramids. What history, mystery lay beneath that lazy benevolent Latin sky. Even the men standing in the rain protected by their raincoats made just from corn husks are picturesque figures and others with their gay serapes around them. Women with their charcoal burners turning and flapping out their tortillas, little girls with a baby strapped across their shoulder, women carrying huge burdens on their heads, balanced perfectly, long burro trains, melons ripening on the roofs, ancient gardens alive with singing birds.

At Cuernavaca, you see the great Palace of Cortez built in 1530! There are the famous Diego Rivera murals and you stroll through the Borda Gardens, favorite resort of Maximilian and Carlotta, his Empress. Taxo is particularly charming, a town right out of a picture book. Its houses rise in tiers on the hillside and its balconies filled with flowers. Its narrow streets slope upward. We had no group with us nor a guide, just a guidebook and as Kathleen spoke Spanish, we were able to get around on our own. The one thing about traveling in Mexico we found was the eternal demand for "tips". You were followed along the streets by ragged little youngsters with their hands out and the one word they had learned to say in English was "teeps" meaning tip. At the hotels one tipped for every favor, too, although they were courteous to the extreme. But all in all, we liked and enjoyed Mexico even with its extreme poverty and its great wealth—those wealthy families who owned the Haciendas—grants of land given back even in 1573—thousands and thousands of acres still being worked (when we were there) by men in white robes, wielding a long spear-like affair and using still a wooden plow. It is different now, twenty-five years later, visitors inform me. Modern machinery is used and those grants of land are being cut up and the little man has been given a chance to make good for himself.

Those days they were no more than chattels. One of those homes contained thirty-five bedrooms.

We planned on a day to go home and that day I sprained my ankle on Mexico's cobbled streets. I had walked miles and miles and the last day finished up with this ankle. But in a few days, I was ready for the journey back to Idaho. We had a better train going back and, of course, were more comfortable. We were awakened at the border about midnight and all had to get up to have their plunder inspected and have their pesos changed back into our money in case we had any left over. Those big husky Americans did look good to us as they boarded our train with their cheery good mornings and big wide American grins. Even Nogales looked good to us as we detrained in the morning; the dwarfed portulacas bright as gypsy shawls in a plot near the depot seemed to welcome us back. We felt as rich as Irish brogue when we counted our money and saw that we could treat ourselves to a good breakfast and some souvenirs. We had been gone twenty-one days and had spent two hundred ninety-eight dollars and fifteen cents, but that was nearly a quarter of a century ago.

CHAPTER VI

Home and Heartbreak

(1939 On-ward)

———————— ◆ ————————

Frank was delighted to have us home again. He had no biscuits, you know, but I had brought home to him real Havana cigars, the best I could find in Mexico City. Lots of work waiting for me—all the late canning, peaches, pears, apples and grapes, so "busy" was the word for me. I had a surprise though, Frank had bought a new Westinghouse refrigerator while we were away and it was the last word in refrigeration. We would look quaint now. Our old one was a wooden affair and as obsolete as a bustle.

Butter had gone up to twenty-five cents a pound and eggs were also twenty-five per dozen, so that was good news. I had been getting fifteen cents for both so times were looking up. Some of our friends were getting radios but we had been invited one evening to listen to one but we couldn't understand a word, so we decided to wait until they were improved. Motion pictures or talking pictures were also popular but we were still using coal stoves and Frank thought we should try the oil stoves to save work. It was cheaper, too, by far than now, but I liked my coal stoves, especially my cookstove in the winter months.

Kathleen was offered a position in the public assistance office and she accepted, as she felt she could try out her social work and if she liked it, would go on training and prepare for it as her future work and career. She at once was put on her own and was doing fieldwork. She didn't say much about whether she liked the work or not so Frank and I were at a loss to know what her future might be. I felt she would not go back to teaching. She stayed with this office and the work for two years and then the state asked her to take special training for child welfare work. She was to go to the Chicago University for two years of training. So again we packed the wardrobe trunk and took our little girl to the train. After two years at home, we missed her.

After she left we began counting weeks until the holidays when she might visit us but it was a long way off, now with airplanes and jets it would not be far. But Chicago, years ago when I first finished my schooling in Dixon, Illinois, I, too, went there but to my first stenographer's job and now my daughter was there. Strange but when I think of Chicago, I yet feel chilly. When I first saw it, a powder of rusty snow hugged the curb, icicles hung like old tears from the eyes of windows. At night the street lights winked at you wolfishly and the first night there was a melon moon and in the dark on the depot platform, for I had to wait till nearly dark for my friends to meet me, cigarettes glowed and died like romantic lighthouses. Kathleen didn't get home until the summer vacation. She loved her work and so

I knew she would never go back to teaching and I was glad, for in this work she had a big field and had worlds of chances to advance in her career. She, too, felt the same way. She went back to her second and last year to get her Master's degree in her chosen work but before the end of that year we were to suffer heartbreak to its uttermost.

Kathleen left in September and in October her father suffered a stroke. He had not been sick, so it came like a bolt out of the blue. I asked Kathleen not to come home as her father, after the first three days commenced to improve and as she had a scholarship in addition to what the state was giving her, I thought it unwise to sacrifice her time and assistance as she would do me no real good by coming home and she would only have the long tiresome train trip back. I nursed him tenderly and patiently and he never wanted me out of his sight. His mind had been affected by the stroke, but he seemed improving each day, until he could accompany me outdoors and watch me raking leaves and putting the flowers to bed for the coming winter. This was October, but by the last week in November, he had another stroke, much more severe than the first, then started to gain a little again and Kathleen had written that she would spend Christmas with us which cheered him immensely as he now had something to look forward to.

The doctor told me that his recovery was very doubtful and to be prepared for a still heavier stroke which no doubt would take him. He kept watching the calendar marking off the days until Kathleen would be with him, but a week before Christmas, he seemed to fail and by the time she arrived, he was bedfast. He would not allow a nurse to be near him so I was with him constantly. Kathleen arrived a day before Christmas and he was overjoyed to see her again. He picked up right away and when her vacation was over, he insisted she go back and finish her year and not to worry about either of us.

She returned very reluctantly and on the 14th of February, he had his last stroke and Frank was gone from me forever. I wired Kathleen not to come back as she had such a wonderful visit with him and I didn't want her to go through all this new grief again. I was stunned and seemed incapable of carrying on but that comes to all of us with a terrible loss by death and I was only one in thousands and I knew I had to carry on, no matter how I felt. I could not ignore the loneliness and if loneliness can be shared, I knew I was not alone. There must be, but does its poignant pain touch others? Lonely like the brightest star out of reach in the sky. Lonely like the far sound of a carol thread in the quiet cloth of a cathedral. Alone as most of us sometimes must be alone with the mystery of his being and his place upon this earth. There is a peculiar thing in the knowledge that we are alone when a loved companion is gone. There is such a void, such an emptiness, you feel your world is finished—you are adrift. I cannot understand nor explain that feeling. I only know that it was so for me and that emptiness has never left me in the twenty years I have walked alone. Frank had left a part of himself to me, a part I must cherish and live for—Kathleen. As long as I had her, he was not really gone. I know that realization saved my reason.

Roy insisted that I now make my home with them but, of course, I refused and said I would start the very next morning with my work on the little home and there was plenty to do, too, with all the fall work not finished and the getting ready for spring. The work was the very best thing for me so I kept busy and in the spring Kathleen came home. The office right in Twin Falls gave her a good position so she could be with me. She had her father's car and could drive back and forth to her office daily and be with me at night. It was wonderful to have her. We had three ranches over in the Jerome country, so they gave me another responsibility to keep them rented, watching the crops and the many responsibilities that go with being a landowner. I worked hard all day and often in the night to get through my tasks but I did it and kept our little home and grounds the way I knew Frank would want them kept. Kathleen stayed with me two years and then had a splendid offer in California, which she could not afford to pass up, so one day she again packed her belongings and I was alone. I thought for a while I just could not stand it alone there on the ranch. She had been such a comfort to me those first two years but again I determined to carry on.

California was not so far away and she could join me or I could go to her nearly every holiday season and she wrote every week. Her headquarters was in San Francisco, a city she had always loved and so that first winter she insisted that we get an apartment and that I come to San Francisco but this first winter it was impossible for I had stock yet on the ranch so we promised ourselves that we would be together the next year during the winter.

The next blow was the death of Ray. My brother, that I had run all the way home from that little country school of long ago, to hold his tiny form. Roy and I were now the only ones left of our immediate family. My next year was an extra hard one trying to adapt myself to do all the work that Frank and I had done together, the heavy shoveling and irrigating, garden and fruit, mowing lawns and clipping hedge. That was all handwork then, as we had no power mowers and electric hedge shears then, but in some way and somehow I managed and went into the winter with everything in ship shape order. My farms across the river into Jerome had paid quite well and I had sold one, too, during the year and that helped.

I had no time for vacation so that in the late fall my dearest friend offered to take me to our famous Sun Valley resort for a few days and this, too, would give me an opportunity to drive through what we called the Hailey timber, where the coloring in the fall was magnificent. The trip was a delight, every minute of it. Sun Valley lived up to its reputation but it was for celebrities and the rich for the prices were high, too high for me, but the trip through the lovely Hailey country was free. The roadbed was a dappled carpet of leaves and sunshine, and we motored like royalty, under a canopy of gold, crimson and magenta. Horses browsed, cantered up and down the fences in sheer joy of living and cattle roamed the field leisurely.

Smoke rose from bonfires like incense and some leaves had settled themselves snugly at the feet of the trees, as if desiring to nourish their mothers in their old age: others hopped and swished across the road as if playing tag with us. The hills spread around in their splotches of bright orange, henna and crimson and here and there a fir tree in their hunter's green. Yards full of late flowers and warm salvia, tipped with flame. The mountain ash had scarlet pincushions at the end of her boughs. All nature seemed to be resting. The maples were all quivering with the soft caressing breeze and bright red leaves were falling from other trees and danced madly along with us. The little gray squirrels flashed here and there like a streak of soft velvet as they scooted up and down the tree trunks, their little round eyes winking roguishly at us.

The branches of the trees creaked solemnly as if protesting at their nakedness. Little faces of the fall flowers looked up at us begging us to pick them so they would not need to curl up and lose their scented beauty when Jack Frost would pinch their soft cheeks cruelly. So we rode along, crossing bridges old and worn even then and enjoyed watching Mother Nature providing for all her children, tucking them away for the winter. She would be there smiling her welcome as they peered out in the spring before bursting out in all their glory later on.

As we turned our car back again to Hailey, the sunset came to add to our enjoyment. She painted the entire west a crimson scarlet with a few clouds here and there tinted a pale pink and yellow with purple splotches here and there like steps down a golden stairway. And one place far above, it looked like a vase of Van Gogh's sunflowers, then the sun's keen eyes closed beneath a brilliant lid of rose and saffron colored sky. I prayed then, I think, that every leaf of memory would be tipped with golden sunshine. Before we reached Hailey, a moon of pale green leaned against the sky at its very horizon. We had a fine day. It made me realize the saying and who said it, I don't recall, "Finds tongues in trees, books in the running brooks, sermons in stones and God in everything."

On our way home, my friend May and I stopped at the ice caves, another interesting spot here in our Idaho. We had to park the car by the roadside and walk through the desert of rock and brush to get to them. Today there is a fine road leading right to them. Here and there was a stake with a white rag on it to mark the way to the entrance. Eventually we came to it, just a hole in the ground, which we had to stoop to get into, and it was the opening to the caves. We very gingerly went down the ladder to the cave itself. We had a lantern with us. It was beautiful as it was entirely lined with ice and the rounded dome above us was ice, glittering like a thousand candles in the dim lantern light. "How could it be?"

We wondered, ice like that right out in the heart of the burning desert. We could hear water trickling somewhere in the distance, but we didn't want to venture too far for if the lantern should go out, we might not be able to find our way back to the opening and anyway, we were chilled through and through. We were happy to see the sunlight and feel the warm air as we came up out of it. They are lighted now with electricity and hundreds of people visit them every summer.

These few days had been a real treat to me and I went back to the ranch and my work with a lightened heart. My work was more or less routine for lawns and hedges had to be taken care of each week. I would just finish watering when I would have to hoe again and so it went with spraying, picking fruit, shoveling ditches in between. I sold my cow and my chickens for I could buy what I needed in that line far cheaper than I could keep the cow and chickens. The horses I had let go sometime before. That lightened my work and, also, made it possible for me to leave in the winter by draining the water out of pipes, etc. You see, I was planning that winter with Kathleen in San Francisco and that came at last as all things do more or less in this life. I had to plan on some new clothes and I had nothing new since Frank died but jeans and shirts and gloves to work in the fields and yard—much more convenient than dresses. Even my ditch rider failed to recognize me when I met him in town with a dress on.

California To Nevada

At last, I found myself California bound. Kathleen met me at the bus station. She was boarding with a fine old Irish woman right up against Golden Gate Park. Kathleen knew San Francisco quite well as she had been at Stanford University for three years and often went into San Francisco. Being there is like being aboard a ship. The sea on three sides of you almost surrounds the city. Buildings rise tall on the hilltops like masts of some romantic freighter, glowing with lights at night against the sky. You'll breathe salt air, too, and fog. Upon the hills you will see how the streets swoop downward to the docks that look like outstretched fingers. You feel the touch of warm ghosts of great events and of vivid colorful people have lingered on in San Francisco, keeping it gay and carefree and friendly and tolerant. You will feel and sense the excitement of San Francisco's turbulent past. Just a village that grew itself into a city by the mad gold rush, bringing in men and women of all races and all religions but they all live with the one desire, to preserve the friendliness and the warmth and glory of the old San Francisco, this romping "gal" who after fires and disastrous earthquakes, rose again to modern greatness.

We visited China town first with all its marvels and queer way (to us) of living and then to Portsmouth Square where Robert Louis Stevenson used to love to sit swapping yarns with the sailors. Jack London loved San Francisco, too. We did the usual things that all visitors do—Fisherman's Wharf, the world-known Golden Gate Bridge, ride on the cable cars and see Mission Dolores and the San Francisco–Oakland Bridge. Think of a bridge eight miles long. Being so close to the Golden Gate Park while Kathleen was at work, I could visit it daily. On Sundays, we planned Seal Rocks, Telegraph Hill and Muir Woods. We decided not to get an apartment so that she would not have the two moves, out and back again and I could board there with her and not cost much more than the upkeep of an apartment. It worked out for the best as I felt that two months was as long as I could stay. Spring comes early in Idaho and ranches then need attention.

I spent some time in Oakland, too, as I had a very dear friend there and she had a car so we went to Berkeley, the site of the University of California, America's largest school. Its library has more than a million volumes, the largest library west of the Mississippi. She took me to Mills College, one of the oldest women's colleges in the United States (1852). The trip to Muir Woods surpassed it all, I think. All about you towers the immense red columns of this redwood cathedral built long ago by God, "*Sequoia sempervirens*" (ever-living). As visitors say, "You can almost HEAR the silence." Your guide will tell you their habits—how they heal their own wounds, survive with their cores burned out like vast deserted chimneys; how the bark is a foot or two thick and almost fireproof; how they have no taproot standing balanced for thousands of years rooted only two to six foot deep, towering to three hundred feet and one that rises three hundred sixty-four feet.

Of course, one can't leave San Francisco without sampling her world-renowned food. When tales of gold began to circulate and men returned from the diggings, sacks bulging with wealth, they had yellow dust to spend for luxuries and it came from everywhere and men lived like kings and "ate like Romans." Chefs from Europe came bringing with them their sauces, their spices and their mysteries of cooking. Rare wines and rare foods were imported and as years passed sons of chefs have also learned to cook for a city that had learned to EAT. They say that along the crisscross of San Francisco's streets, you may order dinner for a thousand nights and never repeat once. I wanted to go at night, for to me the city was more beautiful than any other time. The high towered hills silhouetted against the afterglow of sunset; the lights marching from the valleys to be lost among the stars, the colored lights in jewel–like clusters and the city's nighttime world is gay and invites you to be gay with it. How I wished for Frank to enjoy all this with us.

We had an Italian dinner at Lupo's, I believe. Time went all too fast for me and before I knew it, I was aboard the bus once more, back home and back to work.

The trip had done me a world of good, but the loneliness and the heartbreak was with me still. Roy and friends were urging me to sell the home, as they did not think I should live there alone and that the work was getting too hard for me. But it was home and I just couldn't think of giving it up. It was a part of me now after all the years of living and loving all that time. I sold the farms, though, and that was a start, I guess, in the right direction.

During that summer, Roy's wife heard the fateful news that she had cancer. It was a terrible blow to him and we all did everything that was possible but to no avail and nearly six years after Frank died, she, too, went out into the unknown. Of course, Roy was desolate and as we were the only two left of the family and both alone, he insisted that I sell my home and we two live together with him. In this trial, his greatest, I didn't want him to be alone and suffer the pangs of loneliness that I had.

My sympathy getting the best of my judgment while going out to see him, I did consider selling.

For three months I stayed with him most of the time, going back and forth to my home to water and do the things I just had to do. His son had taken over his farmland and I should have insisted he move in with me, but I didn't. My place had several takers, as it was so beautiful. Kathleen had wanted me to sell it, too, when I was with her, as she thought I was getting too old to be alone especially out in the country. She said she would never be able to make it her home, as her work would always take her elsewhere. So I sold my home and with it went most of me.

Do not be too willing to dispose of the old things—the home you have lived in so long—the barn that sheltered all the newborn things, the wall where wild things bloomed in the warmth of other springs; the swing upon the willow limb with the marks of feet in the earth below—the creaking pump that always had to be primed and the thousand other things that welded all the old scenes into a memory you will never forget. Disposing of an old home is like breaking trust with a friend. How can you tell a perfect stranger, "Now when you come into this room, walk lightly, a little girl was happy here." Or in some nook sheltered and secret which was your hideaway in childhood will you say, "Please don't change this as you may destroy something that was very precious." And how will you dispose of the little gardens? They go with the place! But what of the recollections? Remember the lovely cool nights that you went to these gardens for rest and satisfaction to watch the lovely old moon come up and smile her golden smile upon you, seemingly pleased with what you had accomplished. And what of the tall trees that greeted you each day of your living there with their rustling of leaves like clapping hands, cheering you on to further accomplishments.

What of the memory of the barren limbs in winter, with nests silhouetted against the sky, of its tracery of leaves in summer moonlight and the lovely fairyland after a hoar frost, limbs and leaves strung with the soft snow, looking like chiffon ropes? Trees bending with their lovely burden of white then shimmering like millions of diamonds in the first sunlight. Are you going to be able to forget they're things which you loved so much that your thoughts gave them souls? Will you ever be able to forget the sight of the old road that runs past the place? Of journeys you started through the gateway between the rows of poplars, down the road to happiness—and pain? Will you ever be able to forget the hollow sounds of approaching footsteps as they came to you across the wide front porch? The footsteps that brought their messages of hope, new happiness and tragedy? What of the sight of moonlight spilling in through the front window, turning the brightly patterned carpet and straight-backed chairs into a magical land?

What of the pencil marks behind the bedroom door, placed there in the long ago by baby hands? What of the marks on the white bathroom walls each year marking how many inches that loved one had grown until those marks were five feet six from the floor? What of these things you have sold? Can you place a sign "For Sale" or the fatal one "Sold" on all these things and go marching off with never a backward look—with never a RECALLING? OH. NO. Please don't do it friend! And oh, the mornings that I was always met from the kitchen door, mornings like a golden spoon was spilling out the sun, mornings when the sky was pouting and pulling a blanket over its darkening face and the silver music pattering on the pane, then the wind went wild, then broke down and walked away and evening again came in again with soft feet, then night and the sequined skies glitter. Why do I always remember all these things that I should forget now? SOLD, SOLD, SOLD. I regret it yet. Then the time came for me to move. I did not know where to begin to dispose of thirty-odd years of collecting. I would pack a few things I didn't sell, and when it was all over, I walked down that long drive for the last time, the drive I had raked and dug through snowbanks and trod hundreds of times listening to horses clip-clopping down its length but it was over.

About the time I was settled in Roy's home, his grandson wanted to move into the big house and asked his grandfather to move to the tenant house. I tried desperately to keep his own home knowing how I had missed mine but to no avail when Roy decided to move out into the little house. I bought a little home in Twin Falls and moved my belongings in and once more established a home, but not like the old one. I never again would be content and happy. Time hung heavily now on my hands and my friend, May, who had an antique shop in town asked me to come in and work with her. I did, and grew too much interested in antiques. Here I met many people and my days were pretty well filled up and I was more content.

Of course, I checked up on Roy and had him with me a lot, in fact, asked him to move in with me which he was considering. I knew how lonely and lost he must be in that little tenant house and trying to do his own cooking. A man is far more helpless when they have lost their companion, than a woman is in the same circumstances. I began to be land hungry again and could see possibilities in buying and owning farms in the Jerome country where land was much cheaper than with us on the South side of the Snake River so I became a nuisance to the real estate men, looking at these farms.

I guess they thought I was just a "looker". Frank had been in real estate a long time and as I had worked with him a lot, I felt that I knew land. I found what I wanted and as land was on the upward trend, I knew I could make a bit on the price and then I was to have one-half of the crops, which looked very promising. I was right, for that fall, my part of the crops was two thousand dollars and I sold at an increase of $10 per acre. I was elated. The next four years passed like this with Kathleen coming home at least two times a year. She was glad that I was living in town where I could contact people. Property was advancing and I had a chance to sell my little home for two thousand dollars more than I gave and so I sold again and bought another home close by, still ahead of the game by quite a bit.

In the meantime, I had bought and sold three farms with a crop ahead and a small gain in the transaction of reselling. In my new home, within two years, I had a chance to resell and make eight hundred dollars. Again, I bought a small home at a bargain just three blocks away, so my moving was not much of a problem and by this time I was getting used to moving, "folding my tent and silently stealing away." Our antique business had picked up, too. Our town was getting more modern each day, new folks coming in with money and new ideas. Old things and old ways were quickly passing and I guess, I too, was passing along the way.

May and I had not been on a vacation for some time, so we decided to go to Las Vegas. I had never been to a town like that. Years ago Frank and I drove through there and then it was just a little Mexican cowboy town, a few shacks and mud huts set down to burn in the great desert. Today it is the home of millionaires and movie stars, at least for a few months. It is one big glitter and we wanted to see it. Las Vegas is one of the few spots on this globe where it is possible for the average American, dressed in slacks and sports clothes, to rub elbows at a table with a millionaire, if your ambitions include such a meeting, or if you are just looking for plenty of luxury living, entertainment and excitement at bargain basement prices.

Las Vegas and its surrounding lakes and mountains would be a happy vacation choice. Not many resorts appeal both to families and single persons. Not many resorts offer swimming and skiing simultaneously only thirty minutes apart. Where else can one stay at a motel with a swimming pool for three dollars and fifty cents a night? Las Vegas is a city with hands that play all night and people who never go to bed. That such a city should be where it is at all is a miracle. It is set in sand and cactus, flat with mountains in the distance on both sides. One New Yorker describes it thus: "There's the desert, see. You're driving along with your tongue hanging out, hot as can be. All of a sudden you are in a forest of neon signs spilling out dollars. The bus driver tells you that this is the "strip", two and one-half miles of highway between the airport and the center of town. On the Flamingo Hotel there is a sign shaped like two silos set on end. It fills with silver dollars, the lights go out and it begins all over again. It is a puzzle how Las Vegas can offer so much for so little. One can stay there in an air-conditioned room in luxury for $8 to $12 per couple per day. At one table tourists were slicing away at a huge ham, rare roast beef, turkey and piling on shrimp and lobster Newburg, three kinds of cheese, and several kinds of beans and several fancy desserts—all for one dollar and fifty cents. Second helpings allowed."

Folders describing the place sound almost as fabulous as they are. Everything has been designed with the thought of comfort and enjoyment for the guest. These prices, lush atmosphere and fine food are of course, lures to get the tourist to tarry at the gambling tables where there is activity twenty-four hours a day. No one is forced to try their luck and if a couple will stay away from the gambling tables, they can have one of the most lavish weekends of entertainment, food and atmosphere obtainable in the world for twenty-five dollars! We were more interested in the attractions around Las Vegas than in the gambling.

Hoover (Boulder) Dam open daily to visitors, is only thirty minutes away. There is Lake Mead, the largest man-made lake in the world and is visited by millions of tourists every year. And the Valley of Fire—one can see petrified trees and picture writings of early Indians, scenic and colorful; the valley is nearby and so is Death Valley. Until his death in January in 1954, Death Valley Scotty, ruled this valley. He was a colorful character from by-gone mining days. In it yet, is his famous desert castle and ghost mining town. That year, Las Vegas drew over three million tourists. May and I came back from that little outing ready to buckle down to work again. We did not envy the easy money being made at Las Vegas. We liked our way much better. I was due now for more trouble.

My Time and Place

Roy had died suddenly from a heart attack. The little family bred and born in the little Iowa farmhouse so long ago was all gone but myself. Where had the time gone? How the world had changed since then. We did not operate in any way the same—our food was different, our mode of living not the same, our clothing different, education along different lines, and our whole attitude toward life and its problems was so different. We had gained a lot of "know-how" but it seemed to me we have lost a lot too—the old friendliness, the old neighborliness, individualism and loyalty and sincerity. But who was I to know or criticize?

Kathleen had been given a good position in Boise, our state capital. She was now State Supervisor of Child Welfare, which paid her big money. I think she wanted the position so as to be near me, one hundred and forty miles away, for she dearly loved California. I was glad to have her back in Idaho. This way we could be together a lot for weekends, too. When she was too busy to come, I could spend the weekend with her, which we did often.

Thereafter, I had my last little home five years, I sold out everything and came to Boise to live with my girl. We had a very good apartment, close to her work and close for me to shop. Our life was uneventful there. Then three years ago, I took the trip back to Iowa. Iowa that I told about in the first part of my story. Progress is still marching on and now, in 1960, I have seen the transition from the slow plodding oxen to the marvelous jet plane, with its tremendous speed, office equipment with brainpower surpassing that of the average person, homes automatic, and marvels and miracles performed in medicine and all the sciences, but that is only a start. These improvements and developments within the next fifty years will be outmoded and perhaps obsolete, by the discoveries yet to come.

A vacation to the moon is not impossible for the future businessman and playboy. The housewife will not bother to cook, as all our required food will be in capsule form. There will be spectacular wonder drugs and man-made satellites will circle the globe and war will be no more. You will fly from New York to London in perhaps five hours. Your house will be heated and lighted by the sun and your air-conditioning and refrigeration by the same power. You will learn then that the sun is the eternal power of the whole universe. The Indians were right when they worshipped the sun. Automatic eyes will control your home. Electronic tube cooking will be common in every home, but why cooking if we have the concentrated capsules? And atomic energy will be in use. People are on the move now, a big percent always on wheels or planes but in the next fifty years nearly everyone will have been abroad. Where will the money come from? I guess, too, it will be one of the things we will just remember and dig down for credit cards. We will not see these changes.

Life has been very full for me and I am glad I lived when I did and can look back on a life without tension, worry and hurry. I hope it was not a passive progression from day to day, but an active, stimulating and creative way of living. I am leaving my daughter and I regret to leave her but she is wonderful and has been and is an exceptional daughter. She has never given me a moment's worry or sorrow. She is a success in every way morally and financially.

In youth, we are given vast virgin fields to cultivate and sow as we choose. In awe and wonder, we gaze at our vast estate stretching out before us and we are told that "as we sow we shall reap." We are young and hopeful and dreamingly we plan to sow seeds of ambition, joy, pleasure and kindness. Our intentions are of the best and later the weeds of Greed, Hate, Jealousy, Self-interest, Bad Habits and a host of other deadly noxious weeds creep in and gradually crowd out the plantings of youth which, with constant watching and cultivation, would have brought in a harvest of satisfaction and joy and a knowledge of a full and happy life.

We could then meet old age in the warm golden haze of joys past—an old age like a soft crumbling of shining palaces and memories of shadows cast by a sun nearly set and in the soft whisper of the winds, we would hear the small voice saying, "Well done." May we hold fast and trusting each his own, near the end, with the drawing of the veils and find life refined and drawn by lights of LOVE and HOME, cross the last shoals with flying sails. THIS OUR HARVEST OF YEARS.

I keep thinking of the words of the noted author of St. Louis Blues, in these works and I feel just like that. Remember? "I hate to see de evenin' sun go down." As I sit reviewing my life, I am so grateful for everything that happened—the happy things and they were many and the sad things, too, that I know helped me to live better and gave me the desire to be of help to someone else in time of trouble and only by tasting trouble yourself, are you able to offer love and sympathy and understanding to others.

Now as I sit in the lengthening shadows and glow of the setting sun, I seem to perpetuate the memories yet a little, while fully realizing that so very soon, the shades of time will be drawn and hide them. The coming generations will know them from the pages of a scanty passionless history.

In closing, I give expression to my amazement, gratitude and admiration for my time and place in the world's great program.

Farewell

APPENDIX:

SEPTEMBER 16, 1954

RECOGNIZE HER?—The little girl sitting so proudly on Buffalo Bill's lap is Kathleen Wilson, daughter of Mrs. Iva Wilson of Twin Falls. She is now state supervisor of child welfare. This photograph was taken in September, 1913.

Cochran Family Portrait

(Guy, Wilson, Roy, Iva, Sarah, Ray)

Portrait of Iva Cochran-Wilson

(1876 to 1973)

Portrait of Mary Joan Cochran–Laur

(1930 to 2019)

Acknowledgments

We would like to give a special thanks to Kathy Case whose early efforts are greatly appreciated. Thanks also to the individuals who graciously took the time to review this book, and of course the readers.

Made in the USA
Monee, IL
15 June 2021

71373883R00100